HOW TO
STOP
AND INFLUENCE
PLANNING
PERMISSION

HOW TO STOP AND INFLUENCE PLANNING PERMISSION

ROY SPEER & MICHAEL DADE

JM Dent, London

ACKNOWLEDGEMENTS

We thank the following for their help with the book: Murray Armor for his advice; Kingsley Roger Jones for supplying information; numerous planning officers and civil servants throughout the United Kingdom for providing information; Veronica Humphrey and Rosemary Cook for typing the text; Michael Cheal for supplying Figures 1.5 and 2.3; Ivan Hissey for the cartoons; Alan Hoskins for permission to reproduce his campaign leaflet. Special thanks to our wives and families without whose support the book would not have been written.

NOTE

Names and other details given in some of the examples in this book are for the purposes of illustration only. No reference to real people and places is intended or should be inferred.

First published in 1994 by
JM Dent Ltd
The Orion Publishing Group Ltd
Orion House
5 Upper St Martin's Lane
London WC2H 9EA

Copyright © Roy Speer and Michael Dade 1994

A CIP catalogue record for this book is available from the British Library

ISBN 0 460 86194 8

Printed and bound by Butler & Tanner Ltd, Frome and London

CONTENTS

CHAPTER 5 LOCAL PLANS 88

CHAPTER 6 ROAD BUILDING AND COMPULSORY PURCHASE 108

CHAPTER 7 SPECIAL DESIGNATIONS 121

APPENDICES

INDEX 156

'Another out-of-town superstore is just not required or wanted, and it is time the council realized the fact, before it is too late.'

'It's greed, manifest greed. The developers never seem willing to put in low-cost housing for young couples. We don't need any more executive housing.'

'Our objections to the development proposals remain as strong as ever they were. We intend to support the Local Plan because we believe it is the overwhelming view of villagers that this land is not developed.'

The quotes on the previous page are taken from newspapers, from members of the public concerned about development. In a similar situation what would you do? Could you change anything anyway? How would you go about making your voice heard?

In the 1990s, we are much more aware of the environment – natural and built – and more concerned about environmental issues than we were say fifteen, ten or even five years ago. Few people now are prepared to sit back and let developers and local politicians decide what is best for their communities, yet fewer still have any idea of how the planning system – the system that governs change in our towns and countryside – works and how we can influence decisions on specific develop- ment proposals. As a result, public participation in the planning system is under utilized by those it is there to serve.

But do you as an individual or group have any real power? Objectors to the proposed redevelopment of Kings Cross in London caused five years' delay, cost the developers an estimated £45 million, and the scheme was eventually abandoned. Judge for yourself. Again, controversial plans to build a four-lane trunk road through the 5 hectare (12 acre), 8,000-year-old Oxleas Wood in south London were abandoned by the government after a sustained campaign involving two public inquiries, intervention by the European Community and a series of legal challenges.

Regardless of recent commitments by politicians of all parties to protect the environment, substantial development, based on housing need and job creation, is still programmed. Such development, how- ever, is carried out over many years, so, although you might not be able to stop it taking place, you can still try to influence where it will be located, what form it will take and what can be done to minimize its impact.

For example:

● do you want new development to be built in the countryside or in existing towns and cities;
● do you want town centres to keep their traditional appearance or to be comprehensively redeveloped;
● do you want to see a new road go through a tunnel rather than through ancient woodland?

HOW TO STOP AND INFLUENCE PLANNING PERMISSION is a practical manual that shows you how to take effective action and participate in de- cisions that affect your life. It tells you what to do, where to go and who to speak to. It also discusses what arguments to use and how to set them out in objection letters and statements. This book is not anti or pro development. Our aim is to enable you and other members of the public to influence development decisions by giving a unique insight into the planning system, based on our practical experience of its operation.

People who object to development or who want to have a say are generally not interested in Acts of Parliament or Statutory Instruments; rather, they want to know how to go about making their opinions count. In this guide, therefore, we explain planning procedure only to give a necessary understanding of the system that you will have to use. You can research legal and procedural detail, if that is what you want, in planning law books at libraries and book shops. Government departments, for example, produce booklets summarizing various planning procedures (see page 150), and most are available from council offices. All these books and booklets are useful – as far as they go – but what you need to know, if you are to change anything, are the tips that official publications do not tell you.

HOW TO STOP AND INFLUENCE PLANNING PERMISSION is based on the law in England and Wales. Although Scotland and Northern Ireland are covered by different laws, and terminology varies, their planning systems are similar to those in England and Wales. Any differences are mentioned in the relevant sections of text. Throughout this book, 'his/her' should be understood wherever 'his' appears since planning officers, inspectors and councillors, as well as those seeking planning permission, are as likely to be female as male.

Our book starts by setting the background to the planning system and discusses the factors that influence all planning decisions (Chapter 1). If you are serious about achieving real results, it is extremely important to understand the system and its decision-making basis for your actions to be truly effective. The remainder of the book guides your actions in specific situations such as planning appeals or compulsory purchase orders. No book, however, can give definitive advice on specific cases. If you are ever in any doubt get help from the council, a professional or one of the bodies listed in the appendices (see pages 141–50).

On the whole, individual action on wider questions of national and strategic issues is less likely to be successful.

These might be on the law itself, European or national policies for development, or policies for whole counties or regions. The best way that you can influence these wider issues is to join or support a national pressure group or political party.

Is the planning system so complex that you should not even try to get involved? Are the odds stacked too heavily against you? No. Armed with the knowledge gained from HOW TO STOP AND INFLUENCE PLANNING PERMISSION, you can make a difference. Here are some examples of successful action:

Local groups, with the backing of national campaigners, stopped a council's own proposal for a 3,000 square metre (30,000 square feet) indoor bowls centre being built in Victoria Park, Leamington Spa. The centre would have eroded the historic quality of the park, an essential element of the town's character since 1897.

A 10 hectare (25 acre) colliery, closed for thirty years, at Huncoat, Lancashire was allocated for development in the Hynburn Borough Local Plan. Residents in the area opposed the allocation, and about thirty objections were made to the Local Plan proposal. The council looked at the case again; not only did it decide to remove the development allocation but also the site was designated Green Belt.

Local people living in a tranquil rural area at Northaw, Hertfordshire suffered disturbance from bursts of paintball gunfire and shouting when woodland was used, without permission, for war games. Pressure on the council led to action, stopping the unauthorized use.

Chapter 1

THE PLANNING SYSTEM

The planning system is now such an established part of twentieth-century life that few people question its existence. Planning is not new: the ancient Egyptians, Greeks, Romans, Incas and Aztecs all planned their cities. In the United Kingdom, the planning system has evolved over many years. Some of the finest examples of planned development are those eighteenth- and nineteenth-century estates in places such as Edinburgh and Bath. These predate the formal planning system, which was introduced in 1947, after the Second World War left huge devastated areas of towns and cities to be rebuilt.

The planning system is designed to regulate development in the public interest by providing necessary curbs on free-market development, striking a balance between conservation and exploitation of buildings and land, and reconciling conflicts between private and community interests.

THE SYSTEM

There are currently three layers of government involved in managing the planning system: central government; county and regional councils; and city, borough and district councils (see Figure 1.1). Scotland and Northern Ireland are administered separately from England and Wales. The county council tier of planning administration does not exist in English and Welsh metropolitan areas (Greater London, Greater Manchester, Merseyside, South Yorkshire, Tyne and Wear, West Midlands and West Yorkshire). In these, city and borough councils fulfil county functions. Urban Development Corporations have their own planning authorities, which decide planning applications, as do National Parks (see pages 125–9). There are three regional councils in Scotland which handle all their planning work themselves.

County councils and district councils are sometimes called local planning authorities. For convenience, we use the term 'district council' throughout this book to include city and borough councils. District council areas are divided still further into parish, community or town councils; these we shall refer to as parish councils. Parish councils are consulted and make recommendations on planning applications but have no legal power to decide them. The weight given to their views varies widely. Some parish councils have influence in practice because their recommendations are followed closely by the district council.

Although the European Community does not play a direct role in operating the UK planning system, one of the functions of its Commissioners is to ensure that Community regulations are complied with in EC countries. This led, for example, to intervention by the European Environment Commissioner in 1991 over the M3 extension across Twyford Down in Hampshire. The issue was whether European Community rules on the assessment of environmental effects had been followed.

Planning functions

Planning is divided into two distinct parts: forward planning and development control, and there are opportunities within both parts to bring your influence to bear. Forward planning is done by central and local government to guide future development in an efficient and orderly way. Central government draws up national guidelines, which are translated by local government into county Structure Plans and district Local Plans (see page 13). Development control over individual planning proposals is operated mainly by district councils, which grant planning permission where a proposal complies with policies laid down in the forward planning documents. Some types of development known as 'permitted development' can take place without the need for planning permission (see Figures 1.2 and 1.3). In most cases it is not actually an offence to carry out development without planning permission.

So far we have used the word

11

FIGURE 1.1 OPERATING THE PLANNING SYSTEM

Authority	Personnel	Functions
Secretaries of State for the Environment, for Scotland, for Wales and for Northern Ireland	members of the government and their departments of civil servants	• draw up national policy set out in Planning Policy Guidance Notes, National Planning Guidelines and circulars • oversee the planning systems • decide major planning appeals
Planning Inspectorate in England and Wales; Inquiry Reporters Unit in Scotland; and Planning Appeals Commission in Northern Ireland	planning inspectors/reporters/commissioners	• hold Local Plan inquiries • decide and report on planning appeals
County councils in England & Wales; Regional councils in Scotland	elected councillors and planning officers	• draw up Structure Plans, Minerals Plans and Waste Plans • decide planning applications for minerals and waste • advise district councils
District, borough and city councils in England, Wales and Scotland; Divisional offices, Northern Ireland Department of Environment	elected councillors and planning officers	• draw up Local Plans • decide most planning applications • take enforcement action

'development' in a general sense, but in town and country planning the word has a specific meaning: it covers only building work and changes in the use of buildings and land even though, in the latter case, no actual construction need take place. The term 'developer' strictly means anyone who carries out development but generally refers to anyone who undertakes development for profit rather than for his or her own use or occupation. Throughout this book, we use the term 'applicant' rather

Chapter 2

PLANNING APPLICATIONS

Fundamental to the planning system is the need to get planning permission for most new building work and change of use for buildings and land. Before development begins, a planning application must be submitted to the council for approval. This is the time to stop or influence the proposed development if you are worried by it. Armed with the knowledge gained from this chapter, you have a good chance of influencing the decision.

Most development occurs when planning permission is granted by district councils, yet the general public is generally unaware development is going to take place until construction is underway. By this time it is too late to object; the time to act is during the course of a planning application (see Figure 2.1).

Of the 600,000 planning applications made in the United Kingdom each year, around 80 per cent receive permission to go ahead with the proposed development. The vast majority of these planning applications are for extensions to small buildings, alterations, loft conversions or building a few houses.

You have the greatest scope for involvement and influence while a planning application is being processed. Once granted, you have no right to appeal against someone else's planning permission.

FINDING OUT WHAT IS PLANNED

If you and your community are to make an effective contribution towards planning development in your neighbourhood, you must first monitor the planning applications for development that are being made. These have to be publicized by the council that is going to make the decision by notifying neighbours, displaying site notices and inserting newspaper advertisements.

Immediate neighbours are informed by letter of developments that affect only them. Only in Scotland, however, is a neighbour defined for planning purposes. This definition is relevant for guidance in England and Wales. Neighbouring land is:

● any that directly adjoins the application site or is within 4 metres (13 feet) of its boundaries;
● where a building is divided, neighbours include properties directly above and below both the application area itself and those parts of the building that come within 4 metres (13 feet) of it; and
● roads less than 20 metres (65 feet) wide do not count as part of the 4 metres (13 feet).

If development affects a wider area, or there is doubt over adjoining ownership, a notice is put up on the application site so that it is clearly visible from public roads and paths. Large sites, especially where bounded by more than one road, should have more than one notice. Site notices should be left up for at least twenty-one days. If you see a notice removed or defaced in that period, let the council know straightaway.

Advertisements of planning applications are found in the legal notices section of local newspapers. They are written in semi-legal jargon and appear amongst notices of goods vehicle licences, bankruptcies and council tenders.

Newspapers also run stories in their news sections on significant local development proposals. Parish councils are sent lists of planning applications in their area as, sometimes, are public libraries, Citizens Advice Bureaux, local amenity societies and residents associations. Watch out too for estate agents' boards, especially on undeveloped land. For Sale boards sometimes advertise the fact that the land is being sold for development.

The amount of publicity given to a

for action and precisely what is proposed. Relying on hearsay, which might be inaccurate, can render your objection less effective. Planning applications are supposed to be decided in less than eight weeks of submission. This, however, is a target, not a hard and fast rule.

As soon as you think you might want to object, ask the district council planning department how long you have to submit your comments. This is usually twenty-one days from when the council notified neighbours or put an advertisement in the paper. Meet this date if you can, but all letters received prior to a decision being made on an application should be taken into account by the planning committee.

A copy of every planning application is available for public inspection at the district council's offices during its normal office hours. Council planning departments not open on Saturdays, only a few open in the evening and about a quarter close for lunch. Copies of planning applications can be purchased from the district council. This can be arranged by telephone, although a payment might be required before a copy is sent.

You are also allowed to see previous planning applications and background papers under the Local Government Act 1972. Some officers cheerfully hand you the whole file; others do not. A few councils charge you to look at background papers, which unfortunately they are permitted to do. You cannot be charged for seeing applications, decision notices and planning officers' reports to committee.

Planning departments have receptionists or information officers who deal with the public. Although not qualified planning officers, they are often knowledgeable and in most cases very helpful. Planning officers are usually available to answer queries the receptionist cannot deal with. An appointment might be necessary to guarantee meeting a specific officer.

Some parish councils also have copies of planning applications for the public to see. This might be more convenient but they will not be able to answer questions about the proposal.

UNDERSTANDING PLANNING APPLICATIONS

A planning application comprises a completed application form, a certificate of land ownership, plans and drawings including a location plan, and, in some instances, an environmental assessment. It can be submitted with a covering letter explaining or justifying the proposal.

Application forms

Application forms ask all the basic questions about a proposed development (see Figure 2.2). As you go through the form jot down important facts, any questions you have and points of concern that come to mind. Make sure you have at the very least:

- a note of the name and address of the applicant and agent;
- the address of the site;
- the proposed development;
- the type of application; and
- the council's application reference number.

Forms vary slightly between authorities but these headings are found on most application forms:

FIGURE 2.2 APPLICATION FORM

PLANNING APPLICATION

Please read the accompanying notes before answering each question and write in BLOCK CAPITALS

Date received	22/6/94
Fee paid	£2,880.00
Reference no.	SY/538

1 Applicant
Name and address of applicant
MICHAEL MOTORS
BURTON AVENUE
HAZELDEN
tel no 581 7777

2 Agent
Name and address of agent
HARRISON ASSOCIATES
ST ANDREWS HOUSE
LIMESTANTON
tel no. 671 7846

3 Type of application

Yes/No

a Full application — YES

b Outline application — NO

c Approval of reserved matters — NO

reference no. and date of outline permission...
which reserved matters are included

siting   design   external appearance   access   landscaping

d Renewal of temporary planning permission — NO

reference no. and date of previous permission..

e Removal or modification of conditions — NO

reference no. and date of previous permission..

4 Address of site

Give full address or location. Outline the site in red on location plan

LAND WEST OF PHOENIX HOUSE
PORTLAND ROAD
SANDLEY

5 Description of development

Give full and accurate description of the proposed development

ERECTION OF VEHICLE WORKSHOP AND
STORES WITH OPEN DISPLAY AND
STORAGE AREAS AND PRIVATE CAR
PARKING

6 Area of site

Area of application site........0.5...........~~metres~~/hectares

7 Access and parking

Does the proposal include

a new vehicle access   ✓

b new pedestrian access   ✓

c altering vehicle access

d altering pedestrian access

e provision of parking spaces   ✓

   if so, how many   34

8 Trees

Does the proposal involve loss of trees or affect any trees; if so, indicate trees on site plan

        N/A

9 Existing uses

Described the existing use of the property. If vacant, describe the last use of the site

    DISUSED ROWING CLUB

10 Drainage

a How will foul sewage be disposed   PUBLIC SEWER

b How will surface water be disposed   THROUGH INTERCEPTOR TO RIVER

11 Materials

For new building work, state type and colour of all external materials (walls, roof, surfacing, fences). Show materials on application drawings

    COATED PROFILE SHEET STEEL, TARMAC SURFACING
    WALLS DARK GREEN, ROOF BEIGE

12 Plans

List all plans and drawings included as part of the application

    LOCATION AND BLOCK PLAN   FLOOR PLANS AND ELEVATIONS

13 Signature
Read and then sign the statement
I apply for planning permission for the development described in this application, and shown on the accompanying application drawings. I enclose a fee of   £2,880.00

Signed   *M. J. Harrison*   Date   17th JUNE 1994

On behalf of   MICHAELS MOTORS

Reference number

This is usually written prominently on the form by the council when the application is registered and should be used on all matters connected with the application.

Applicant

This is the person making an application or on whose behalf it is made. The applicant does not necessarily own any or all of the land, or have the owner's permission to make an application, and he or she can conceal their true identity by using a false name. Planning permission relates to the application site, not to the person who makes the application. Applications can be made with the intention of selling with planning permission.

Agent

Where an applicant appoints an agent, the council corresponds with him or her, rather than the applicant. An agent is any representative who acts for an applicant. Just because an agent is used does not necessarily mean that person or firm is qualified or even knowledgeable. Planning consultants are often used as agents, as sometimes are estate agents, solicitors, architects and builders.

Type of application

There are two basic types of planning permission: full and outline. A full application shows all the detail of planning proposals, while an outline application establishes the principle of development, leaving details – the reserved matters (siting, design, external appearance, access and landscaping) – for subsequent submission to the council. (Details of the reserved matters should be submitted within three years of the outline planning permission but these do not have to be on an application form.) Applications for changes of use, engineering operations and mining cannot be made in outline.

The full/outline/reserved matters distinction is important when you frame your objections or comments. For an outline application, you should deal with the general concept or principle of development, such as whether this is the right place for the proposal. Check carefully what details are reserved in the application. Usually all are, but not necessarily. The form should specify this. If the application is for approval of reserved matters, you will not be able to challenge the concept of development. This will have been established earlier when outline planning permission was granted. Your comments in this instance should be directed to the submitted details, which should be consistent with the outline planning permission. On a full application, you can comment on both principle and detail.

Planning applications can be made to vary or remove conditions on earlier planning permissions or to renew temporary planning permission. Ask at the planning department to see the previous application. Look at the decision notice, officer's report to committee and any other information on the file to find out why the condition was imposed in the first place. See whether anything has changed. On an application to renew temporary planning permission, you need to look at the existing development to see what problems there have been and whether permission should be allowed to continue.

Address of site

Addresses given can be vague, especially when the proposal is on open land, for example 'land west of London Road, Silsby'. Check that other people who might be concerned about the application will realize where the site is from the address given. It is this address that will be in any newspaper advertisements and lists of applications.

Description of development

This section contains the most important information on the form. The description determines what is applied for and, if approved, what has planning permission. Some descriptions are clear, simple and brief, for example, 'four detached houses'. There would of course be garages, drives, fences and garden buildings as well as the houses themselves. If the application is in full, you can check these details on the plans. Other descriptions specify every single element of the proposal; this can obscure the true nature of the application.

Area of site

The figure given should correspond with the area edged with a red line on the location plan. If density of development is an issue, check the calculation of site area yourself.

Access and parking

See whether a new access is proposed, as this can have an impact on appearance, highway safety, traffic generation and pattern of traffic routes. If parking is proposed, compare the number of spaces with the council's standards.

Trees

Application drawings should show which trees on the site would be affected by the development. Check whether any are protected by Tree Preservation Orders (see pages 122–4).

Existing uses

Any activities taking place or that have taken place and any rights to use the site could be crucial to the decision. As planning history/existing uses can be highly relevant to a decision, this sometimes induces applicants to misdescribe or exaggerate the answer to this question on an application form. Your own local knowledge, asking around in the area or looking up the site history at the planning department might clarify the true situation and provide vital information for your objection.

Drainage

Before planning permission is granted, authorities ensure the development can be properly drained. The absence of available public or private sewers, unsuitability of land to cope with a private treatment system, insufficient capacity at sewage treatment works and overloading of existing sewers can stop planning permission for development.

Where buildings or hard surfaces are included in an application, rain or surface water has to be disposed of. Constructing a building might mean a different distribution of rain and so reduce the amount of ground over which it can drain away. This can cause problems in boggy ground, poor draining soil and areas with a high water table. Surface water goes to public surface water drains, soakaways (drainage pits in the ground) or existing water courses (ditches, streams, rivers).

Materials

Full applications should state the style and colour of the proposed external materials. Such details are especially important in Conservation Areas and near Listed Buildings.

Plans

Some forms ask for a list of plans and drawings submitted with an application. With outline planning applications, applicants can submit illustrative drawings, but these should be clearly marked as they do not form part of the formal application. They can nevertheless be important as they show how development might look or prove that it can fit on a site.

Revised drawings can be substituted while the council is dealing with an application. The drawings stated on the form might not be the ones on which a decision is finally made. If in any doubt check with a planning officer.

Signature

Forms are signed and dated by applicants or their agents. The eight week target period for determining applications runs from receipt by the council, not from the date on the form. Delay in submission and registration of applications can occur. Most planning applications require a fee, the level of which depends on the type of planning application.

Commercial and industrial development applications must have an additional form, from which much useful information can be gleaned. You can:

● check car parking standards against proposed floor areas;
● see what loss of particular uses such as shopping or industry there would be;
● gauge activity from staff numbers;
● judge the impact of vehicle movements from the numbers given; and
● find out what processes are involved.

There are separate additional forms for agricultural development and mineral extraction.

Certificates of land ownership

Sometimes a certificate of ownership is included in the planning application form; at other times a separate form is used. Applicants must state whether they own the whole application site, whether anyone else owns the site or part of it, and whether any part is included in an agricultural tenancy. Owners for this purpose include anyone with a lease of seven years or more. Make a note of the owners' names and addresses in case you want to contact them later.

Plans and drawings

Look at the location plan carefully: Ordnance Survey maps, on which most location plans are based, can be out of date. A location plan sometimes misses off buildings, especially recent development, and neighbours can find their properties or recent extensions are not shown, for example. Make a note to point out any inaccuracies to the planning officer. A location plan should identify the application site clearly in red and show adjoining properties and roads. All new

FIGURE 2.3 TYPICAL DRAWINGS TO ACCOMPANY A PLANNING APPLICATION

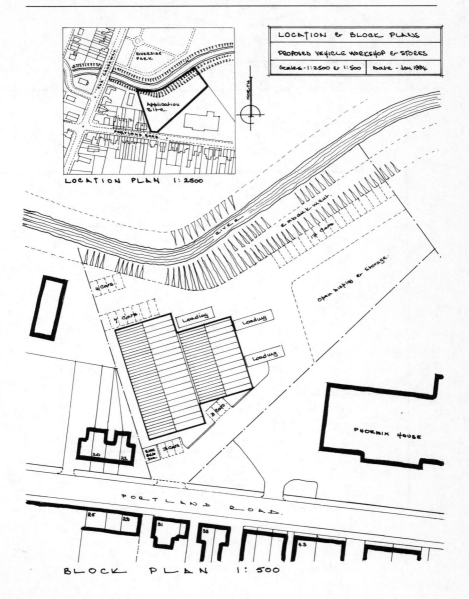

LOCATION PLAN 1:2500

BLOCK PLAN 1:500

FIGURE 2.3 (CONT.)

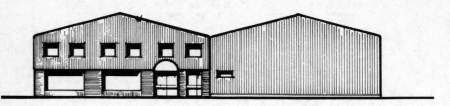

SOUTH ELEVATION

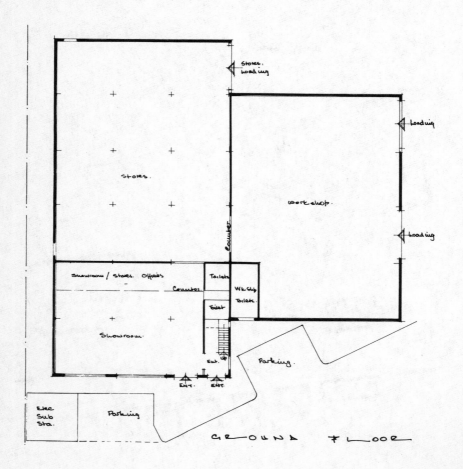

GROUND FLOOR

FIGURE 2.3 (CONT.)

EAST ELEVATION

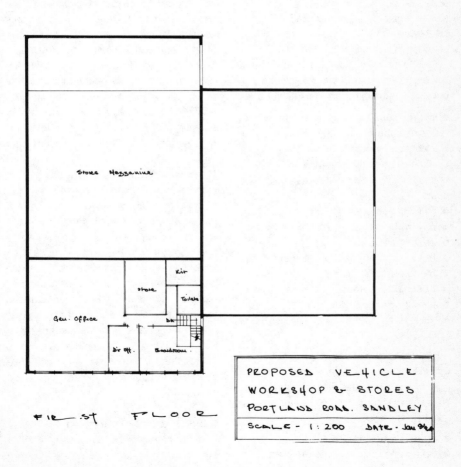

Stores Mezzanine

Kit

Store

Toilets

Gen. Office

Dk

Dir Off.

Boardroom.

FIRST FLOOR

PROPOSED VEHICLE
WORKSHOP & STORES
PORTLAND ROAD. SANDLEY
SCALE - 1:200   DATE - Jan 96

buildings and areas in which a change of use is sought must be within that line (see Figure 2.3). If the applicant owns or has control over other land nearby, this should be outlined in blue. Blue-edged land is important because the council can impose conditions on planning permission relating to other land the applicant owns. Public rights of way cannot be diverted without separate permission, so check the drawings to see what effect a proposed diversion might have.

Get a photocopy of the location plan to take away with you, or make a note of site boundaries and adjoining property.

Planning applications for new buildings and alterations will include site or block plans. These should show:

● boundaries, existing and proposed, including subdivision within the site;
● existing and proposed buildings;
● buildings on adjoining land;
● roads, pavements, verges and footpaths;
● existing and proposed accesses;
● any works proposed to public highways;
● parking areas;
● trees and other natural features;
● proposed landscaping;
● existing and proposed drains, sewers, cesspools, septic tanks; and
● uses to be made of undeveloped parts of the site.

In addition to site plans, full applications include floor plans as well as the front, back and side views of buildings. These drawings, which show design and layout, include:

● materials and finishes;
● colour and texture of the exterior;

● changes in ground level;
● construction of access; and
● position of doors, windows, loading bays.

Interpreting drawings and visualizing them in three dimensions in the proposed setting is not always easy although extensions and alterations are often shaded to help distinguish them. Nor is cross-checking separate drawings of the existing and proposed buildings. Check distances to boundaries, distances between buildings, heights of buildings and floor areas with a scale rule. You might need to spend some time studying drawings in order to understand the proposal fully or ask a planning officer to go through the drawings with you. Make notes as you go, jotting down any inconsistencies, inaccuracies, doubts or concerns.

Environmental assessment

Planning applications for a limited number of projects – only a few hundred each year – need an environmental statement on the effects a proposed development would have on the environment. This is then assessed by the council. Such environmental statements should have a non-technical summary and it is to this that you should refer unless you have a great deal of time or expert knowledge. Make notes and base your comments on this information. Alternatively, if you have funds, get specialist expert help (see Appendix I).

Covering letter/statement

If there appears to be no covering letter or statement with the application, ask a receptionist or planning officer whether a letter was submitted – it can easily have become detached from the forms and plans.

Applicants' statements usually contain valuable information mostly, of course, in support of the proposed development. Such information helps you understand an application better and might even allay some of your fears. Beyond this, it can provide you with more ammunition or allow you to refine your arguments.

As you go through the letter or statement note points you disagree with, inconsistencies with the forms and plans, aspects you do not understand and points that you need to check, such as any history and Local Plan policies referred to.

INSPECTING THE SITE

Some points to note when studying a planning application relate to physical factors on and around the site – relationship to nearby properties, safety of access, loss of trees and many others. Unless you are very familiar with the site, go and have a look at it. Take your notes and make a thorough investigation, bearing in mind the points you wrote down.

Even if the site is well known to you, it is still worth walking around the area. View the site from all angles and from all vantage points. Jot down where the proposed development could be seen from, what would be seen next to and near it, and what it would be seen against – trees, buildings or sky.

Photographs can be very useful reminders of particular details and features of the site and its setting and they can be included as evidence with your objection.

OBJECTIONS

People concerned about planning applications rarely think to contact the person, agent or organization making the planning application, but this can produce results. Councils only have power to say 'yes' or 'no' to a proposal or modify it to some extent by conditions. It is applicants who draw up proposals and they generally prefer these not to be the subject of formal objections in case this sways the planning committee.

You have to gauge for yourself whether it is appropriate to contact a particular applicant. Some are indifferent to opposition; yet many are keen not to upset people, especially if they live and work in the community or if they are concerned about public image and bad publicity.

If you decide to speak to the applicant, do it as quickly as possible, so that the application can be revised or you still have time to get an objection to the council. It is particularly worthwhile contacting the applicant if your objection relates to a detail in a proposal, such as the position of a window or the effect on some natural feature. The scheme could perhaps be altered without it being affected overall.

Adopting a friendly rather than a combative approach increases your chance of being listened to and achieving success. If the applicant is unwilling to talk, concentrate your efforts on the planning officer or councillors instead. If the applicant agrees to make changes, ensure the planning application is formally amended before a decision is made. Do this by checking with the planning department in plenty of time before the planning committee meeting.

Where an applicant does not own the

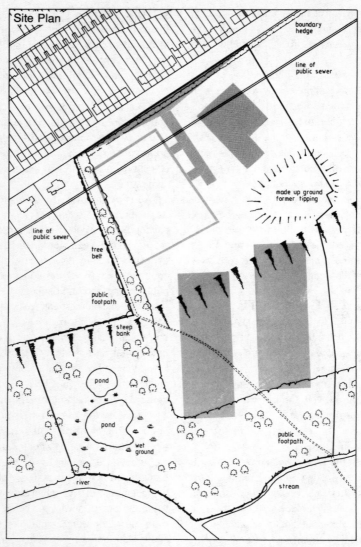

Site Plan

boundary hedge

line of public sewer

made up ground former tipping

line of public sewer

tree belt

public footpath

steep bank

pond

pond

wet ground

public footpath

river

stream

When inspecting the site, you should consider the following points illustrated in this proposal for new buildings, car park and access: effects on houses; loss of boundary hedge to create access and visibility splay; building over public sewer; loss of trees; effect on remaining trees; effect on, and diversion of, public footpath; contamination from former tipping; visual impact of construction across change in ground level; effect on wildlife around ponds; pollution of river and stream.

application site you can contact the owner. He or she might know very little about the proposed development and might be concerned that it is attracting opposition or that it might be harmful in some way.

Meeting the planning officer

A planning application is assigned to a planning officer, or sometimes to a team of officers, whose role is to assess an application and to write a report on its merits, culminating in a recommendation for approval or refusal of planning permission by the district councillors. Decisions on planning applications in Northern Ireland are made by the Divisional Planning Officer, not by district councillors.

Find out the name of the planning officer assigned to the planning application in which you are interested and arrange a meeting. If this is not possible, speak to the officer on the telephone, or better still ask him to come to you. At the meeting have paper and pen handy to record what is said. Referring back to your notes on the planning application, ask the officer to explain points you do not understand. Tell him if you think you found inaccuracies or errors. If you feel an application lacks sufficient detail discuss this with the officer, as councils can ask applicants to supply additional information. Explain what worries you have about the proposed development and why. Listen carefully to what the officer says: you could be mistaken about some aspects. It might be that, in this particular case, the council has no choice but to grant planning permission.

Ask the planning officer which plans and informal planning policy documents are relevant to the proposal. He should be able to show you the documents and point out which sections and individual planning policies apply. Write this down for future reference.

Remember when you are talking to the planning officers that they are limited in their realm of activity. They are not concerned with other types of control – vehicle operators' licences, water supply, off-licences, environmental health rules – nor with private legal matters such as disputes over land ownership, boundaries and co-venants. Always be polite and courteous. A sympathetic planning officer can be a very useful ally so try to get a good rapport going and stay in touch with him.

Get the officer's views on what you can do about the application and do not dismiss his advice lightly – yet you should not let yourself be put off if you are not convinced. Even at an early stage the planning officer can often give you a good idea of what the recommendation is likely to be. Remember that, although the recommendation is important, it is the councillors who actually make the decision and they are not bound to follow their officer's advice.

Planning departments have a hierarchy of officers (see Figure 2.4). Try to establish the position in the hierarchy of the officer you talk to. Just because an officer appears sympathetic with your concerns or even agrees with you entirely, that view does not necessarily prevail. Planning officers always maintain they are completely independent of elected councillors, yet this is not always true. The degree of independence varies between authorities.

FIGURE 2.4 DISTRICT COUNCIL PLANNING DEPARTMENT PERSONNEL

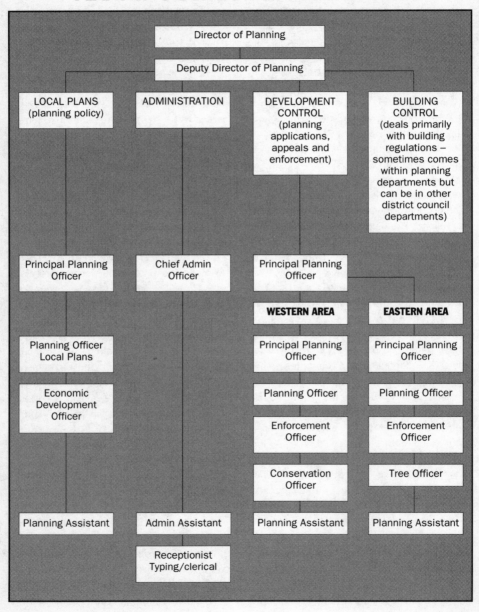

Contacting councillors

Since it is councillors who make up the planning committee and who ultimately decide the planning application, they are the people who need to be convinced of your case for influencing a planned development. Sometimes a single councillor speaking forcefully at a committee meeting can turn the tide of opinion. What would otherwise have gone through on the nod can, through a councillor's intervention, be refused or conditions insisted upon. Even if a planning officer recommends a refusal, do not presume the planning application will definitely be turned down: an applicant might have been working hard on councillors, and so it is up to you to do the same.

Most planning applications are not actually discussed at committee meetings, since there are likely to be twenty to fifty applications on any agenda, and so the officer's recommendation is accepted. It is the minority that are talked about.

Some twenty to thirty councillors will be on a planning applications committee, and some councils have more than one planning committee. These can be split geographically or just divided into two or more groups to spread the workload.

If you have any personal contacts on the council speak to them first and ask people in the area to find out if they have a friend who is a councillor. Contacts in political parties or local organizations could introduce you to a councillor. Otherwise, get the name, address and telephone number of council members from the district council, together with a note of those who sit on the planning applications committee. Most councils produce year books listing councillors' names, addresses and political affiliations, various committees and dates of committee meetings. It is best to contact councillors who are actually on the planning committee, although if your local councillor is not, he or she might still take an interest as might the councillor for the area in which the application is located. In Northern Ireland councillors do not make decisions on planning applications but are consulted, and there is a procedure for resolving cases in which the Divisional Planning Officer and district council do not agree.

Lobbying councillors can sometimes prove counterproductive and needs to be done with care. Try to contact them at times likely to be most convenient – at their weekly surgeries, if they hold one, or during office hours or early evening. Do not overdo it: harassing councillors will not help your case, so avoid getting into an argument if your opinions differ.

Make your contact early and do not be surprised if, especially when an application has only just been submitted, a councillor is not aware of the proposal. He is not likely to be familiar with the detail of an application, unless his attention is drawn to it specifically. Tell the councillor what the application is about, give him the reference number, and explain why you are concerned. Be diplomatic: perhaps ask what his views are before explaining what you think is wrong with the proposal. Try asking for his advice on who else to contact and what else to do. If there might be a political angle on the application, let the councillor know. For example, where the controlling group on the council is backing a proposal, the opposition might make political capital by taking up the case against. Planning committees occasionally hold site visits, so if you think it would be helpful to your case, ask the councillor to press for a committee site visit. This is also likely to delay a decision on the application and give you extra time to get support for your campaign.

Conclude your conversation by asking what the councillor will do. Usually he will investigate the application and speak to a planning officer. If you occupy a property next door or near the application site, invite the councillor round to see things first hand. Follow up your initial contact close to the planning committee date to discover the latest information and try to cultivate the councillor's goodwill. This is especially useful if you want to object to a number of different planning applications as it can give you an insight into how the council will react to proposals. As an alternative to meeting the councillor, ring him up or write. Avoid writing a long letter; stick to one side of a single sheet of A4 paper if at all possible. Councillors are generally busy people and a long detailed letter might not be read at all. Summarize your concern with a few brief points and possibly attach a copy of your letter of objection.

Do not be shy about getting in touch with councillors. They are elected to serve the community and to represent the local electorate's views. You will find most councillors diligent and sympathetic, even in cases where they cannot help you.

Letters of objection

Once you have studied the planning application, been out to the site, spoken to the planning officer and, possibly, contacted the applicant and/or councillors, you should possess the raw material needed to make your objection or comments suitably convincing.

An objection in writing is read and considered by the planning officer, noted in the officer's report to committee and put on the application file. That file is not publicly available until the time a decision is made, when it can be read by members of the public, including the applicant.

Before you write your letter, get clear in your mind precisely what it is you object to. For example, you might be opposed to particular uses wherever and whenever they are proposed – nuclear facilities, gambling or slaughterhouses. Alternatively, a development proposal could be acceptable to you, in general terms, but you believe the site chosen is not the right place for it – wind turbines in a National Park, scrap-metal yard near a residential area, housing on an attractive open space in a town or a road through a Site of Special Scientific Interest. In other cases, you might not be opposed to the development in principle or the chosen site, but you do object to one or more aspects of the particular scheme put forward – poor design, excessive scale, access badly sited, damage to trees, hours of use or problems of overlooking.

The scope of your arguments depends upon the type of application being made (see page 28). Consider whether your objection is to some detailed aspect that could be overcome by the council imposing a condition on a planning permission. Conditions could cover protection of trees, use of certain building materials on the outside

FIGURE 2.5 AN EFFECTIVE LETTER OF OBJECTION

District Planning Officer
Fletton District Council
Remington Street
Thatton   17 March 1994

Dear Sir

PLANNING APPLICATION REFERENCE AT/4/94
LAND TO THE REAR OF CHURCH ROAD, PENFOLD

I wish to register an objection to this application for industrial units. The reasons for my objection are as follows:

1 Planning Policy

The proposal conflicts with policy H3 of Fletton District Local Plan. This requires new industrial development to be sited away from existing residential areas. The site is partly in a residential area.

Part of the site protrudes into the countryside, beyond the 'Built-up Area' boundary line shown on the Local Plan proposals map. Countryside policy EMP9 specifically states; 'applications for new industrial development will not normally be allowed outside the Built-up Area'. There is no special justification for the proposal in this case.

2 Planning History

The site was used as allotments until four years ago and never has been a 'car storage yard' as stated on the application form. There is no history of industrial use on this site.

3 Site Layout

The proposal represents over-development of the site. The layout is very cramped. It would involve the removal of a mature oak tree which contributes to the character of the area. This tree is not shown on the application plans.

There is inadequate vehicle manoeuvring space on the site. There are only three car parking spaces shown and this does not comply with your council's parking standards.

4 Effect on Neighbouring Property

The industrial units include first floor offices whose windows would overlook the rear of houses and back gardens in Church Road, removing our privacy completely.

5 Effect on Surrounding Area

The proposed buildings are of a stark, industrial design and out of character with the brick cottages of Church Road. The development would intrude into open countryside to the rear of Church Road. They would be prominent, especially from the adjoining public footpath, and visually damaging in the landscape.

The development would attract commercial traffic on to Church Road, which is a narrow residential road. The access is near a bend so that increased traffic movements and additional on-street parking would create safety hazards.

6 Conclusion

This proposal conflicts with Local Plan policies, would create traffic hazards and would be wholly out of place in this residential road. Privacy at the rear of our houses will be lost. The severity of the overlooking problem can best be appreciated from my back garden. Please come and look for yourself when you visit the site.

A number of my neighbours object to this proposal and will be writing to you independently. We believe this application should be refused as it would be entirely inappropriate and harmful in this location.

Yours faithfully

FIGURE 2.6 AN INEFFECTIVE LETTER OF OBJECTION

17th March 1994

Dear Sir

I was shocked and dismayed to read of the development plans next door to my house. Surely it is time to put a stop to this sort of thing before the whole countryside is swallowed up in one huge industrial estate. The developer is obviously only in it for the money. HE MUST BE STOPPED!

I have enjoyed my views for 15 years and these eyesores will ruin it. Why oh why does this sort of thing have to go on? I can only guess that someone at the council is putting something in their pocket to let it through!

Just think of the mud and mess. We have already had the road up three times and we simply will not put up with more disruption. If they must build industrial buildings, surely they can put them SOMEWHERE ELSE. I will be speaking to my MP.

Yours faithfully

of a building, limiting the number of storeys or closing an access. There are limits on what conditions can achieve, however, so raise this with the planning officer.

Bear in mind planning applications occasionally offer opportunities to clean up or improve land and buildings: allowing development on part of a site can mean the remainder is landscaped. The reuse of a derelict building might mean it is repaired, maintained and kept secure so it might be preferable to accept the development while trying to limit its impact and pushing for benefits.

How you write your letter and what you say are a personal matter but here are a few tips to help to give your letter of objection maximum impact (see Figure 2.5). Such tips might appear obvious but you would be surprised how many people elect not to follow them (see Figure 2.6).

When writing your letter of objection, do:
● use the notes you made when studying the planning application;
● limit your comments to the actual development proposal concerned;
● base your arguments on known facts;
● back up your assertions with evidence where you can;
● concentrate on planning issues (see Chapter 1);
● explain why the proposal would be harmful and to whom;
● make your points as brief and concise as you can;
● be as specific in your claims as you can;
● type the letter if possible; failing that, write very clearly; and
● quote the application reference number and address of application site.

Do not:
● exaggerate the likely effects of the proposal;
● make personal remarks about the developer or his motives;
● limit your comments to your own personal interests and concerns;
● make assumptions as to the applicant's intentions;
● include factors unrelated to the use of land, such as the value of your property (although the reasons why your property would be devalued may be relevant);
● make unsubstantiated claims;
● use emotive generalizations (e.g. 'we've had enough development'); and
● underline, use capital letters or exclamation marks in the text.

A full and comprehensive letter of objection to a planning application should include some or all of the following topics (see Figure 2.7). There could also be others you can think of and use in addition to:

● planning policy;
● special designations;
● planning history;
● site considerations;
● neighbours;
● surrounding area;
● miscellaneous.

Planning policy
The Local Plan provides the basis for most decisions (see Chapter 5). Study it at the district council planning department or local library, or buy a copy from the council.

Look up relevant issues – housing, employment, traffic, environment and others – that the planning officer men-

FIGURE 2.7 GROUNDS FOR OBJECTING

Planning policy   conflict with Structure Plan and Local Plan policies
contrary to government planning policy guidance
not complying with council's informal policy guidance
prejudicing comprehensive development of an area
exceptional personal circumstances

Special designations   loss of important Tree Preservation Order trees
'inappropriate development' in Green Belt
harm to landscape of National Park or Area of
 Outstanding Natural Beauty/National Scenic Area
threat to wildlife or geological features of Site of Special
 Scientific Interest
conflict with character of Conservation Area
damage to historic or architectural value of Listed Building
harmful to the setting of Listed Building
destroying archaeological remains or monuments

Planning history   losing important socially beneficial uses
reducing housing accommodation in area of housing
 shortage
other applications refused and no change in circumstances
contrary to inspector's views in previous appeal decision
incompatible with existing planning permission

Site considerations   overdevelopment
insufficient garden or amenity land
lack of private space
excessive bulk or scale
introducing unnatural features
spoiling natural or existing contours
incompatible with the design of existing buildings
loss of important trees, hedges or other vegetation
threatening a public right of way
insufficient parking spaces
failure to meet council's access and on-site turn-in standards
loss of important wildlife habitats
harm to rare plants or animals

destroying traditional field patterns
loss of high-quality agricultural land
public sewers inadequate
risk of flooding or creation of flood risk
threat to health of occupants through previous
    contamination

Neighbours
overlooking adjoining properties
blocking natural daylight
generating noise, disturbance, smells, pollution
unsociable hours of operation

Surrounding area
dominating nearby buildings
conflict with the pattern of development
poor relationship with adjoining buildings
visually damaging in the landscape or in the setting
conflict with the character of the area
environmental damage caused by vehicles
inconvenience for pedestrians
road system is inadequate
prejudicing highway safety
loss of open spaces
losing historic street pattern
adverse effect on rural economy
adverse effect on economy and businesses
loss of employment or traditional industries
threat to viability and vitality of town centre
creating imbalance between jobs and homes
failure to meet housing needs
better alternative sites available

tioned or the applicant referred to in the planning application. Find the application site on the proposals map. There might be a specific policy relating to the site or to the area; if so, see what it has to say. Local Plans generally show areas where the councils think that various kinds of development are or are not appropriate.

In your letter refer to policies that are relevant and support your contentions. Say in what way the proposed development conflicts with the Local Plan. If you can, add why that would be harmful in this particular case. Also, ask the planning officer if there are any relevant informal policy documents giving general guidance or a development brief on site development. If there is any relevant informal policy, see how the planning application measures up and point out any conflicts with that policy in your objection letter.

Special designations

Ask the planning officer or see for yourself whether the site is covered by a special designation such as Area of Outstanding Natural Beauty, Green Belt, Conservation Area or Listed Building (see Chapter 7). In most cases any such areas are shown on the map in the Local Plan. If the proposal affects a Listed Building check that a separate Listed Building consent application has been made. In deciding planning applications, the effect the proposed development would have on trees covered by a Tree Preservation Order can be important (see pages 122–4). The loss or threat to protected trees is a valid reason for objecting to development proposals, although such trees are not sacrosanct and a balance with other factors must be made. The age, species, health of trees, the contribution the tree makes to the appearance of the area, the distance to proposed buildings and compatibility of the development with nearby trees all have a bearing.

In the Local Plan read through the sections on development in specially designated areas. These point out particular features and might help guide your thinking on the effect the development being proposed would have on the area.

Planning history

While you are at the planning department studying the application or Local Plan, ask to look up the planning history of the property. Some councils have record cards for each property, which show the date and council's reference for each application, what decision was made (refusal or approval) and the date of the decision, and whether an appeal was made against the decision together with the outcome.

Potentially, any previous planning decision can provide useful material for objections: for example planning permission for a similar scheme might have been refused and possibly a subsequent appeal dismissed. This does not create a legal precedent however, and a subsequent scheme will not automatically be turned down. Ask for the file on any rejected application and see why it was refused and if the current proposal overcomes previous objections. Try to establish whether there are any other changes in circumstances.

Previous planning permissions, even when they have lapsed, can tie a council's hands in making its decision: for example, the suitability of the site for the development could already be established. See what differences there are between these previous planning permissions and what is now put forward. The applicant could be keen on securing a few more units or a bit more floor space. The arrangement or layout could be different. Some new buildings may have been erected since the previous planning permission was granted or a new Local Plan might have come into force with different policies.

In your objection letter it could also be advantageous to mention the type, nature and level of existing use of the site as these can be relevant to a decision, especially if this differs from that stated by the applicant.

Site considerations

In your objection letter, describe briefly the existing features of the site, such as shape, slope, trees and vegetation, and boundaries, then go on to say how they would be affected and the harm that would cause both to the specific site and to the area. You can attach photographs to your letter to help make or emphasize a point.

Neighbours

Looking at your notes on the application drawings and notes you took at the site, try to visualize the effect the development will have on neighbours. Think too about likely effects of the use – noise, increased activity, smells and pollution.

If you are actually a neighbour yourself, resist the temptation to exaggerate or to be emotional. Be objective and specific: if, for example, you are concerned about noise or losing natural daylight, say which properties have windows facing the application site and what the rooms closest to the development are used for.

Surrounding area

Refer to the notes you made on site and describe briefly the setting of the application site, its prominence, its relationship to other buildings and uses, and the road network. Then say what the effect of the development would be. If you feel a proposal would spoil the area, say what is significant about the land or buildings concerned, and what would be affected, and how seriously. The affects could be visual, health, safety, noise, employment, housing conditions and many others. Use photographs to illustrate views from various points and the nature of nearby properties.

Miscellaneous

There may also be technical grounds on which to challenge a planning application: for example, the correct notices have not been served or the application is not in the correct form. Unless you are very sure of your ground, technical points might best be discussed with the planning officer rather than included in your formal objection.

Finally, if you think the application is inaccurate or there are omissions, suggest the planning officer might care to satisfy him or herself that the plans are accurate or that certain facts are correct or whatever the case might be. Do not condemn the applicant. Occasionally, planning applications are made in languages other than English. If possible, offset any advantage this might give the applicant by getting your letter translated into the same language.

When you are happy with your letter, take a photocopy for your records. Then, send the original to the planning department, quoting the planning application reference number.

MOBILIZING SUPPORT

In theory, weight of numbers against a proposed development is not in itself relevant to the planning merits of an application for planning permission. In practice, councils can be swayed by public opinion and pressure. Some applications are turned down partly, and some only, because of public opposition – councils preferring to turn down an application and let a planning inspector take the decision on appeal.

If you do decide to enlist support, keep your objectives firmly in mind. The three groups of people who can stop development at the planning application stage are applicants, councillors and the Secretary of State and it is these you must influence. Whatever you do, always be responsible in all your actions.

Make a list of those affected by the development and who else might oppose it, using your notes on the planning application. Your local library keeps lists of local organizations such as amenity societies, residents' associations, wildlife and architectural conservation groups, and chambers of trade and commerce, together with contact names and addresses. Residents in Hildenborough, Kent got good support from horse riders in opposing a waste disposal site. The access lane was used by 200 local riders, whose safety would have been threatened by heavy lorries.

Planning a campaign

Your immediate objectives are:

- to alert others to the proposal;
- to get across the harm it would cause; and
- to let others know what they can do about it and when.

Start with the people you know – friends, neighbours and others in the area. Check who the planning department notified about the application and how. Where a site notice is put up, make certain it stays up and in a readable condition for the full twenty-one days.

Make up your own notice, preferably on brightly coloured card with large letters. Neighbours and local shops could perhaps be persuaded to display one, but you should not put up this notice on anyone else's land without their consent.

Compile a leaflet and, if resources allow, get it designed and printed. Delivering leaflets can be effective, but relate their number and distribution to the type of proposal and the areas it would affect. Almost half those notified by leaflet of a road proposal in West Sussex responded to this form of publicity. To achieve maximum results, attach or include as part of your leaflet a form for people to complete or just to sign and send to the council, or possibly to the applicant. Of the 2,700 objections to the Kidderminster, Blakedown and Hagley bypass, 90 per cent were made on postcards distributed by Friends of the Earth. A leaflet can also double as a handbill to give out to people in the street.

Organize a petition. Even though the fact that someone objects to a development does not in itself carry much weight, councillors and applicants could be influenced by popular opposition. A petition of 14,500 signatures was collected as part of a successful campaign to stop a thirty-bed hotel and fifty time-share units at Millers Dale in Peak National Park.

Get in touch with local newspapers, which are hungry for good news stories. Telephone journalists at the papers and try to get them interested in writing an article on the proposed development. Such stories are the staple diet of many regional and local papers. Supply them with the

This excellent example of a leaflet to get support was sent to households by the Action Group for the Preservation of Village Life. It explains the proposal, gives the importance of the issue, tells people how to register their views and states the timescale for action. The campaign persuaded 2,600 people to write to the council – the largest number of letters it had ever received.

basic facts about the application – where the site is, who is applying and who is objecting, what is proposed, when it is to be decided, and why you object. Local papers like using quotes from local people, so offer to supply these too, with of course the consent of the people you quote.

Contact local radio and television stations if the proposed development is of wider interest than just the immediate vicinity. Again, give them all the relevant information. Tell them about the effect of

the development on the area and the level of opposition. If you are very lucky and can involve a national or local celebrity in your campaign, this virtually guarantees media coverage. The involvement of writer and actor John Wells in opposing an extension to a quarry near his home close to the South Downs secured an article in the *Daily Telegraph*.

If the scale of the scheme is sufficiently large, national newspapers could cover the story – as they did when campaigners successfully stopped a trunk road through ancient woodland at Oxleas Wood, Eltham. Write to the editor of the paper for the letters page, keeping your letter brief: most letters published are less than 300 words. Anything longer is liable to get edited, and it is better you ensure the salient points are included in a short letter.

Arrange a public meeting and invite the press. Meetings in themselves attract publicity and interest and can generate enthusiasm for a wider campaign. The parish council or a local group might provide a hall or even help organize the meeting. Invite speakers such as councillors, planning officers, someone who knows about planning and, if appropriate, the applicant or his or her agent. At the meeting agree tactics, coordinate the campaign, delegate action and organize fund raising. Ask whether other objectors are willing to contribute money to a campaign. Use funds for getting professional help (see Appendix I) or printing leaflets, posters, T-shirts and badges. Appoint spokesmen or coordinators who can meet applicants, councillors and planning officers on behalf of all objectors with greater authority. You have more clout with a body of people behind you.

In all your efforts to inspire others to action, tell them specifically what they need to do and when. Make sure they know when the decision is to be taken and periodically check this date. Urge other objectors at least to write to the council.

National campaigning organizations

National campaigning organizations, pressure groups and other bodies might take up your cause, depending on the issues involved. Some, such as the Councils for the Protection of Rural England and Wales, Open Spaces Society and the Friends of the Earth concern themselves with development generally. The Open Spaces Society coordinated objections against proposals by Eton College for a 2.4 kilometre (1.5 mile) long rowing trench in the Thames Valley. Others such as the Royal Society for the Protection of Birds, Victorian Society, Ramblers Association and Campaign for Real Ale (CAMRA) are concerned with development affecting their specific interests. The Victorian Society and CAMRA, for example, objected to an office block that would have meant demolition of the 200 year old Tommy Ducks pub in Manchester. (See Appendix II for names and addresses of some campaigning organizations.)

Make contact with any relevant group as early as possible, giving it all the details you have about the application and urging it to become involved. It might even know about the planning application already through its routine monitoring of development. National campaigners have representatives experienced in opposing development proposals, so stay in touch with them and coordinate your efforts. Do not sit back and leave opposition entirely to them as they could change their minds or not make all the points you want to put forward. Regard their involvement as a useful addition to your own action.

Becoming a decision maker

You, or your group, could be concerned about development generally in your area and the sort of decisions your council is making. If so, think about getting direct power by standing for election to the district council; rather than relying on others, you will then be making the decisions yourself. Objectors in Walton on Thames, Surrey formed the Residents Party when Elmbridge Borough Council sold the town hall and open space for redevelopment. They won nineteen council seats against Conservatives twenty-three, Liberals ten and Labour eight and this put them in a powerful position to decide planning applications.

Contacting consultees

When a planning application is submitted, the district council consults various organizations that have responsibilities, or knowledge relevant to, or are affected by the proposed development. Consultees include:

● other district council departments such as environmental health and leisure;
● county/regional councils;
● parish councils;
● highway authorities, drainage authority;
● English Nature, Scottish Natural Heritage, Nature Conservancy Council for Wales, Environment Service of Northern Ireland DoE;
● English Heritage, Historic Scotland, CADW (Welsh Historic Monuments Executive Agency);
● government departments such as the Department of Transport and the Ministry of Agriculture, Fisheries & Food;
● National Rivers Authority;
● National Trust, National Trust for Scotland;
● local police; and

● British Rail, British Coal.

Ask the planning officer who has been consulted and, if appropriate, find out what comments such consultees make. Responses to consultation start coming back to the district council about a month after the application was submitted to the council.

In most cases it is not appropriate or necessary for you to contact consultees direct. However, if you are particularly concerned about an aspect of a proposal, get in touch with the relevant consultee. You might just be able to alert his or her organization to something, perhaps a local factor, which could affect the response back to the district council. Where consultees are particularly alarmed by a proposal, they can become active objectors themselves.

Ask the consultee for information relevant to the proposed development or where you can find sources of more detail. Note what he says and add this to your letter of objection to the district council, refining your arguments and making them more precise.

A parish council's opinion on a planning application can be significant, not least because many parish councillors are also district councillors and parish council recommendations are often followed closely by the district council. In any event, they have personal contacts on the district council and could influence them, so contact local parish councillors. Approach them in the same way as you would district councillors (see pages 39–40). Discuss the planning application and let them know your views.

Lobbying Members of Parliament

The local Member of Parliament does not have a direct role in planning decisions yet in some cases, through political connections, he might have influence with district councillors. Letters from Members of Parliament to the planning department carry no more weight than letters from members of the public.

Lobbying the Secretary of State

The Secretaries of State for the Environment, for Scotland, for Wales and for Northern Ireland have the power to take the decision out of a district council's hands by calling-in applications that would affect wide areas, be controversial nationally or in the region, conflict with national planning policy and where national security or foreign governments are involved. Examples of called-in applications include:

● Scottish Nuclear – dry spent fuel store at Torness, East Lothian; and
● Paternoster Associates – six buildings accommodating 7,700 square metres (77,000 square feet) of offices and 15,000 square metres (150,000 square feet) of shopping in the setting of St Paul's Cathedral.

The call-in powers are used rarely – about 135 a year in England, fifteen a year in Scotland, ten a year in Wales and eight a year in Northern Ireland. If you are concerned about a proposal, you could write to the appropriate Department of Environment regional office, Scottish Office, Welsh Office or Northern Ireland DoE head-quarters urging the use of the call-in procedure. The more people who write, the more chance there is of the application being called-in. However, you will need to weigh up whether the Secretary of State is more likely to refuse the application than the district council. This can happen in cases where the council itself is making or promoting a planning application. Of called-in decisions made during 1991/92 about a third were given planning permission.

Lobbying regional councils

In Scottish regions where district councils handle planning applications, a regional council can call-in planning applications but only if they are significantly contrary to a Structure Plan or where important new issues are raised. If an application matches these criteria, contact a planning officer at the regional council or try speaking to a regional councillor.

THE DECISION

You can see the planning officer's report on a planning application (see Figure 2.8) a few days before the relevant meeting and get a photocopy. Ask at the planning department for the date, time and place of the meeting, which will be open to the public. Double check that applications that you are concerned with are on the agenda.

If you have spoken to councillors who have promised support, let them know you are going to attend the committee meeting to hear the discussion. They might then speak more forcefully on your behalf, because at most committee meetings neither applicants nor objectors are

FIGURE 2.8 A TYPICAL PLANNING OFFICER'S REPORT TO COMMITEE ON AN APPLICATION

Address	Land adjoining 52 East Drive, Bucklegate
Proposal	Outline, Erection of five luxury cottage-style detached houses
Application number	AN/94/0245
Applicant	AB Builders Ltd
Consultations	*Adj properties:* six letters received, all object, overdevelopment, loss of trees, dangerous access. *Petitions:* one, attached. *Bucklegate Conservation Group:* object, over development out of keeping with attractive low density residential area. Protected trees at risk. Two houses would be acceptable. *Borough Engineer:* removal of frontage hedge required to give adequate northerly visibility.
Policies	Borough Plan policies: H2, H3, and ENV7 Structure Plan: no conflict Conservation Area: not applicable

Site description The application site extends to 0.5 acres of level grassland. It is bounded by established hedgerows on the east and west boundaries and close board fence on the north and south. There is a group of three protected oak trees in the south-east corner.

Site history Previous application for three pairs of semi detached houses refused, 1987.

Comment Housing development is acceptable in principle on this site. However the cramped form of development proposed is out of character in this low density area. The development, if permitted, would have an incongruous and uncomfortable relationship to the existing pattern of development, contrary to Local Plan policy H2. Although only in outline, concern is expressed over the likely proximity of the rear houses to the protected trees. If permitted, the location of the dwellings could give rise to an application to fell the trees that would be difficult to resist. Due to the size of the access required to serve the development, the frontage hedge must be lost to meet the visibility standards of the Borough Engineer. This proposal has met with unanimous objection from local people and is considered unacceptable.

Recommendation	Refusal
Reasons	1. Overdevelopment, contrary to Local Plan policy H2
	2. Adverse effect on landscape, policy ENV7
	3. Unneighbourly, poor relationship to existing development

allowed to speak. You can only sit in the public seating and listen. Have paper and pen handy in case anything said is worth noting for future reference.

Some councils, including Calderdale Metropolitan Borough Council, Hastings Borough Council, Maidstone Borough Council, Portsmouth City Council and the London Borough of Richmond, allow members of the public to speak at committee meetings. In Scotland, objectors to applications that are contrary to council's plans have the right to speak. Find out well in advance whether your council has such a policy. Ask what the procedure is and how long you can have to speak. Think whether you actually need to speak. If your other action has been effective, there is probably no need.

Since the planning officer's recommendation is accepted without discussion on most applications, the one that you have gone to hear may or may not be discussed and will be decided with or without a recorded vote. Where the committee is divided a formal vote is taken, usually following a discussion of the application.

If you cannot attend the committee meeting, you can find out the result of a planning application by telephoning the planning department the day after. In England and Wales, councils do not have to notify objectors of decisions, although some do. In Northern Ireland, the Divisional Planning Office notifies objectors of its decisions. In Scotland, councils send decision notices to all objectors. Where planning permission is given contrary to planning policy, Scottish councils should also send out reasons for granting permission.

Four planning decisions are possible: permission; delegated; deferred; and refusal. We look now at the implications of each.

Planning permission

Planning permission gives the right for a development to go ahead. Look at the decision notice, which is usually available within a week or so of the committee meeting, to see whether permission is subject to conditions and what they are (see Figure 2.9). Discuss conditions with a planning officer if you are in any doubt about their effect. In some cases there will be a 'planning obligation' controlling the development or requiring the applicant to do something (see page 17).

Delegated decisions

Decisions are sometimes made in principle but, for technical reasons, not formally made. This happens where:

● a consultation period has not expired;
● further information unlikely to affect the decision is awaited;
● the council wants revised drawings showing amendments to the scheme; or
● a 'planning obligation' is to be signed by the applicant before planning permission is given (see page 17).

The formal decision is delegated to the most senior planning officer to make when the outstanding matter is resolved. Contact a planning officer a couple of days after the committee meeting to discover what is happening with a delegated decision. There might be opportunity for further lobbying or action before a final decision is made.

FIGURE 2.9 A TYPICAL DECISION NOTICE GRANTING PLANNING PERMISSION

ROSELAND DISTRICT COUNCIL

APPLICATION NO.   FG/94/875

TOWN & COUNTRY PLANNING ACT 1990

APPLICANT: Mr D Metcalfe, Barley Street, Upton

AGENT: Philips & Partners, Western Road, Boxbridge

DESCRIPTION: Conversion and extension of buildings to six craft
                    workshop units

ADDRESS: 24 Commercial Way, Upton

In pursuance of its powers under the above Act, the council hereby GRANT planning permission for the above development, in accordance with your application received on 1/2/94 and the plans and particulars accompanying it.

Permission will be subject to the following THREE CONDITIONS:

1 The development hereby permitted shall be begun before the expiration of five years from the date of this permission.
Reason: To comply with the requirements of section 91 of the Town & Country Planning Act 1990.

2 Prior to the commencement of the development hereby permitted, a schedule and samples of materials and finishes to be used for the external walls and roofs shall be submitted to, and approved in writing by, the local planning authority.
Reason: To secure a satisfactory external appearance in the interests of amenity.

3 Access shall be to Commercial Way only. The existing access to Cromwell Lane shall be stopped up, prior to commencement of the works.
Reason: In the interests of highway safety.

Dated: 1 April 1994

Signed:

DIRECTOR OF PLANNING
For and on behalf of the council

Deferred decisions

Decisions are deferred in similar circumstances to delegated ones, but where the committee wants to make the final decision itself. Applications are often deferred where committee members decide to make a site inspection. This normally means they are uncertain whether planning permission will be approved or refused, so more lobbying might prove useful, as with delegated decisions.

Refusal of planning permission

Refusal of planning permission might be what you seek but is not necessarily the last you will hear of the proposed development. Check carefully the reasons given for refusal on the decision notice (see Figure 2.10). If these are for some detail or technical deficiency, the applicant might amend the design, find a new access point or scale a scheme down. If an applicant appeals, the reasons for refusal usually define the main issues disputed at appeal.

There is nothing to prevent a revised planning application being submitted a day, a month or a year after refusal.

COMPLAINTS

You can complain to the Local Government Ombudsman, if you feel the council handled a planning application badly, treated you unfairly or failed to follow procedure properly. The Ombudsman, however, will not look into the merits of a planning application and cannot alter the decision. Complaints are referred to the Ombudsman by the council, or if the council refuses you can make the complaint direct (see page 145). You can get a booklet on how to go about making a complaint.

Planning-related cases accounted for a quarter of complaints made in 1991/92, and maladministration was found in about 3½ per cent of the total number of complaints made. Very few cases are pursued beyond the preliminary stage.

PLANNING APPLICATIONS – ACTION CHECK LIST

1 Check with the district council whether a planning application has been made.
2 Ask when comments are supposed to be submitted and when the application will go to a committee for a decision.
3 Study the application, visit the site and make notes.
4 Meet the planning officer to discuss the application and continue to monitor progress.
5 Contact councillors.
6 Write your letter of objection and send it to the council.
7 Alert other potential objectors and the media.
8 See the planning officer's report to the planning committee.
9 Attend the council's planning committee meeting to hear the application discussed, or telephone for the result.
10 Look at the council's decision notice.

FIGURE 2.10 A TYPICAL DECISION NOTICE REFUSING PLANNING PERMISSION

HARDING BOROUGH COUNCIL

REFUSAL OF PERMISSION

TOWN AND COUNTRY PLANNING ACTS

Application Number:	KG/94/1253
Applicant:	Bowring Construction
Situation:	SITE AT BARN LANE, KIRKWOOD
DESCRIPTION:	CHANGE OF USE TO STORAGE OF BUILDER'S MATERIALS

In pursuance of its powers under the Town and Country Planning Acts, and all other powers, the Council hereby refuses to permit the development specified in the plans and application specified above, for the following reasons:

1. The development would represent an undesirable commercial use of the land detrimental to the amenities and outlook of nearby residents.

2. The form and use of the development proposed would be out of character with surrounding properties and visually damaging in the street scene.

3. The proposed development would result in an unacceptable loss of preserved trees to the detriment of the character and amenity of the area.

4. The position of the proposed access does not accord with highway safety standards. Impaired visibility at the new junction would present a hazard as would additional traffic movements from stopping turning and manoeuvring vehicles.

Dated: 25th March 1994

To: Marshal & Co
       Marine Parade
       Kirkwood

Signed:
Borough Planning Officer

Chapter 3

APPEALS

Where planning permission is refused by a district council, only the person who made the planning application can appeal for the decision to be reconsidered. Appeals are made to the Secretary of State for the Environment, the Secretary of State for Scotland, and the Secretary of State for Wales and the Planning Appeals Commission in Northern Ireland. An applicant can also appeal if a district does not decide a planning application within eight weeks of its receipt. Each year there are around 30,000 appeals in Britain. About one-third of these appeals result in planning permission being granted.

Appeals are dealt with in one of three ways:

● written representations, in which appellants (applicants who appeal) and councils put in statements of their cases;
● informal hearings, in which appellants and councils discuss issues in an appeal in front of a planning inspector, or inquiry reporter in Scotland; or
● public inquiries, which are like court hearings but less formal, with an inspector, reporter or commissioner as the judge.

About 85 per cent of appeals are decided by written representations, the remainder being split equally between informal hearings and public inquiries.

Planning appeals take decisions on development proposals out of the local scene. There is less scope for lobbying, and public opinion is less influential in appeals. Your action here needs to be fought squarely on planning issues. You should not, however, feel daunted by the semi-legal appearance of the appeals process. The public has a role and, if you want to make your views count, do not hesitate to get involved.

FINDING OUT ABOUT PLANNING APPEALS

It is difficult to predict which applications are likely to be appealed. Applicants might make it clear at the application stage that they are prepared to appeal. The larger the scheme and the more money that was put into the application, the greater the likelihood of an appeal. Applicants weigh up the reasons for refusal given by councils and decide whether an appeal stands a chance of success. The cost of fighting appeals can put off applicants.

Appeals are not publicized as widely as planning applications. If you commented on the original planning application, you should be notified when an appeal is made. Your objection letter to a planning application is sent to the inspector and will be taken into account automatically. Organizations that were consulted during the original planning application are also notified. You should be notified separately of the time and place of a public inquiry, if there is to be one. When public inquiries are held, the person appealing puts up a site notice giving the time and place.

District councils keep records of appeals submitted. Local papers often run stories about significant appeals but do not rely on this. Ask the planning officer who dealt with the application to make sure you are contacted if an appeal comes in. The safest way to find out if an appeal has been submitted is to double-check periodically with the district council. If you are concerned with one particular planning application, a monthly telephone call to the district council should suffice as appeals have to be made within six months of the original planning refusal.

The public has twenty-eight days to comment on an appeal. Comply if you can, although any letters received before the appeal decision is taken are still taken into account. An outstanding appeal does not stop a new planning application being made so watch out for this. Applicants sometimes appeal to put pressure on councils while trying to negotiate a planning permission.

STUDYING THE APPEAL

Go to the planning department and ask to see the file and the notice of appeal forms, quoting the planning application reference number. If you did not see the council's decision notice or the planning officer's report on the original planning application, start with them and look at the reasons given for refusal on the notice. These are the basis on which the appeal is fought. See what the officers said about the proposal in their report. Buy photocopies or take notes. Then study the notice of appeal itself. The appeal form is well laid out and straightforward, divided into seven sections, A to G (see Figure 3.1). Appeal forms in Scotland and Northern Ireland are divided into numbered sections but the information required is exactly the same as in England and Wales, except in Northern Ireland the person making the appeal does not give grounds of appeal.

Check the name of the appellant (an applicant who appeals) is the same as on the original planning application as only applicants can appeal. Note which method of appeal – written representations or public inquiry/hearing – the appellant has opted for.

Where appellants ask for written representations, the council can insist on an inquiry. Councils cannot insist on written representations where appellants want an inquiry. In most cases, councils go along with written representations.

Ask the planning officer whether the council is to insist on a public inquiry. If it is not and you feel a public inquiry would give you a better chance to get your views across, speak to councillors very quickly.

Overall some 33 per cent of appeals result in planning permission being given, yet for appeals decided by public inquiries the figure is higher, at around 44 per cent. The council states whether it agrees to the written representations procedure in an appeal questionnaire, which it should complete within fourteen days.

On the appeal form, check that you have seen the documents and plans referred to and make a note of the grounds of appeal so that you can deal with the points in your letter or statement.

Then read the council's appeal questionnaire, noting whether there are any special designations, such as Conservation Area or Green Belt, and which planning policy documents and specific policies the council says are relevant. Write down the appeal reference number if you do not have it already.

An appeal statement may or may not accompany the other appeal documents. Even if it has not yet been submitted, you should write your letter of objection straightaway. If necessary, follow up with a further letter when you see the statement. If you want to comment on the appellant's statement, ask the planning officer handling the appeal to let you know when the statement arrives at the council – but do not rely on this.

When you get hold of a copy of the appeal statement, read the appellant's case carefully and make notes. There is no set form for appeal statements, clarity and quality varying widely depending on who writes it. Check factual points; note anything you disagree with. Look closely at any new plans or drawings since limited scope is allowed to revise proposals

FIGURE 3.1 APPEAL FORM

The Planning Inspectorate

An Executive Agency in the Department of the Environment and the Welsh Office

Planning Appeal to the Secretary of State
Town and Country Planning Act 1990
Town and Country Planning General Development Order

FOR OFFICIAL USE ONLY

Date received

The appeal must reach the Inspectorate within 6 months of the date of the Notice of the Local Planning Authority's decision, or within 6 months of the date by which they should have decided the application.

A. INFORMATION ABOUT THE APPELLANT(S)

Full name: RESIDENTIAL RENTALS LTD

Address: 45 COAST ROAD

SEASIDE

Daytime Telephone number: 783 2352

Postcode: SE37 2FR   Reference: sk/lv.102

Agent's name (if any):

Agent's Address:

Daytime Telephone number:

Postcode: Reference:

B. DETAILS OF THE APPEAL

Name of the Local Planning Authority (LPA): SEASIDE BOROUGH COUNCIL

Description of the development

CONVERSION TO 20 SELF CONTAINED FLATS

Address of the site: NOS 26-30 GEORGIAN SQUARE

SEASIDE

Postcode:

National Grid Reference (see key on OS map for instructions).
Grid Letters: Grid Numbers
eg TQ: 298407

HS 846 : 111

Date and reference no. of the application in respect of which you are appealing.   11/5/94   SE/1150/94

Date of LPA notice of decision (if any).
18/7/94

(REV 1993)

FIGURE 3.1 (CONT.)

C. THE APPEAL

THIS APPEAL IS AGAINST the decision of the LPA:-

1. to *refuse/~~grant subject to conditions~~, planning permission for the development described in Section B. ☑

2. to *refuse/grant subject to conditions, approval of the matters reserved under an outline planning permission. ☐

3. to refuse to approve any matter (other than those mentioned in 2 above) required by a condition on a planning permission. ☐

Or the failure of the LPA:-

4. to give notice of their decision within the appropriate period on an application for permission or approval. ☐

*Delete as appropriate

D. PROCEDURE

1a. Do you agree to the written procedure? (ie an exchange of written statements with the LPA and a visit to the site by an Inspector). If yes, please tick opposite and answer question 1b below. ☑

OR

1b. Tick if the whole site can clearly be seen from a road or other public land. ☐

2. Do you wish to appear before and be heard by an Inspector? (ie at a local inquiry or hearing). If yes, please tick. ☐

E. SUPPORTING DOCUMENTS

A copy of each of the following should be enclosed with this form.

1. The application submitted to the LPA; ☑

2. Any Article 12(A) certificate (site ownership details) submitted to the LPA; ☑

3. Plans, drawings and documents forming part of the application submitted to the LPA; ☑

4. The LPA's decision notice (if any); ☑

5. Other relevant correspondence with the LPA; ☑

6. A plan showing the site in red, in relation to two named roads (preferably on an extract from the relevant 1:10,000 OS map) ☑

Copies of the following should also be enclosed, if appropriate:

7. If the appeal concerns reserved matters, the relevant outline application, plans submitted and the permission; ☐

8. Any plans, drawings and documents sent to the LPA but which do not form part of the submitted application (eg drawings for illustrative purposes); ☐

9. Additional plans or drawings relating to the application but not previously seen by the LPA. Please number them clearly and list the numbers here .... ☐

F. APPEAL CERTIFICATION

IMPORTANT: THE ACCOMPANYING GUIDANCE NOTES SHOULD BE READ BEFORE THE APPROPRIATE CERTIFICATE IS COMPLETED.

SITE OWNERSHIP CERTIFICATES

PLEASE DELETE INAPPROPRIATE WORDING WHERE INDICATED (*) AND STRIKE OUT INAPPLICABLE CERTIFICATE

CERTIFICATE A

I certify that:
On the day 21 days before the date of this appeal nobody, except the appellant, was the owner (*see Note (i) of the Guidance Notes) of any part of the land to which the appeal relates.

OR

CERTIFICATE B

I certify that:
I have/*The appellant has* given the requisite notice to everyone else who, on the day 21 days before the date of this appeal, was the owner (*see Note (i) of the Guidance Notes*) of any part of the land to which the appeal relates, as listed below.

~~Owner's Name~~   ~~Date on which notice was served~~

Signed ___Residential Rentals ltd___ (on behalf of)

Name (in capitals) ___RESIDENTIAL RENTALS LTD___   Date ___18/8/94___

AGRICULTURAL HOLDINGS CERTIFICATE (TO BE COMPLETED IN ALL CASES)

* None of the land to which the appeal relates is, or is part of, an agricultural holding.

OR

* ~~I have/The appellant has given the requisite notice to every person other than my/himself-self who, on the day 21 days before the date of the appeal was a tenant of an agricultural holding on all or part of the land to which the appeal relates,~~ as follows:-

~~Tenant's Name~~   ~~Date on which notice was served~~

*Delete as appropriate. If the appellant is the sole agricultural tenant the first alternative should be deleted and "not applicable" should be inserted below the second alternative.

Signed ___Residential Rentals Ltd___ (on behalf of)

Name (in capitals) ___RESIDENTIAL RENTALS LTD___   Date ___18/8/94___

FIGURE 3.1 (CONT.)

G. GROUNDS OF APPEAL If the written procedure is requested, the appellant's FULL STATEMENT OF CASE **MUST** be made - otherwise the appeal may be invalid. If the written procedure <u>has not been requested</u>, a brief outline of the appellant's case should be made here.

1   THE HOUSES ARE PHYSICALLY SUITABLE FOR CONVERSION WITH INTERNAL ALTERATION. EXTERNAL ALTERATIONS, INCLUDING NEW DORMER WINDOWS AND EXTERNAL STAIR CASE, WILL NOT ADVERSELY AFFECT THE APPEARANCE OF THE BUILDING. OTHER PROPERTIES IN THE TOWN HAVE BEEN CONVERTED.

2   TARMAC SURFACING OF THE FRONT GARDENS WILL PROVIDE SOME CAR PARKING SPACES. THERE IS IN ANY EVENT ADEQUATE ON STREET CAR PARKING AVAILABLE IN THE EVENINGS. MOST FLATS IN THE TOWN CENTRE DO NOT HAVE THEIR OWN CAR PARKING SPACES.

3   THE SCHEME WOULD NOT RESULT IN NEIGHBOURING PROPERTIES BEING OVERLOOKED TO AN UNACCEPTABLE DEGREE. THE FLATS WOULD NOT GIVE RISE TO ADDITIONAL NOISE AND ACTIVITY.

4   POLICY R17 OF THE BOROUGH LOCAL PLAN SAYS THAT IN APPROPRIATE CASES FLAT CONVERSIONS WILL BE ALLOWED IN THE CENTRAL AREA. THE PROPERTY IS CLOSE TO ALL THE TOWN CENTRE FACILITIES. THERE IS A SHORTAGE OF HOUSING IN THE AREA, PARTICULARLY SMALL UNITS.

continue on a separate sheet if necessary

PLEASE SIGN BELOW

I confirm that a copy of this appeal form and any supporting documents not previously seen by the LPA has been sent to them. I undertake that any future documents submitted in connection with this appeal will also be copied to the LPA at the same time.

Signed   _Residential Rentals Ltd_   (on behalf of) _____

Name (in capitals)   RESIDENTIAL RENTALS LTD   Date   18/8/94

CHECKLIST

- This form signed and fully completed.

- Any relevant documents listed at Section E enclosed.

- Full grounds of appeal/outline of case set out at Section G.

- Relevant ownership certificate A, B, C or D completed and signed.

- Agricultural Holdings Certificate completed and signed.

Send one copy of the appeal form with all the supporting documents to:

The Planning Inspectorate
Tollgate House
Houlton Street
Bristol BS2 9DJ

A copy of the appeal form **must** be sent to the LPA at the address from which the decision on the application (or any acknowledgements, etc) was received, enclosing only copies of those documents not previously seen by the LPA.

between planning applications and appeals. If the original application was for outline planning permission, completely new or different drawings can be submitted, so consider the effect of revisions. See what is said about the council's reasons for refusal and, if you objected to the original application, check whether these points are addressed. Speak to a planning officer about any aspects that you do not understand. Then study the council's statement on the appeal to give you ideas and guide your thinking.

Councils' and appellants' appeal statements are generally produced late in the appeal timetable, sometimes not until just before the inspector's site visit (see page 69). Do not miss your opportunity to comment by waiting to see these statements.

OBJECTIONS

It is sometimes possible to negotiate with the person making the appeal. Similar considerations apply as when approaching him about a planning application (see page 35).

The names and addresses of the appellant and agent are on the appeal form. If the appellant is willing and able to meet some or all of your objections you need to ensure the scheme is amended formally. A new planning application could be required for significant amendments. Sometimes a revised application can be approved before a decision on the appeal is made and ideally the appeal should be withdrawn by the appellant.

Where amendments are relatively minor, revised drawings can be substituted in the appeal documents or new conditions

suggested. Bear in mind that whilst you, the appellant and the district council might agree on amendments and conditions, an inspector is not compelled to do so. If you have any doubts about amendments, check with the planning officer.

Meeting the planning officer

The planning officer assigned to handle an appeal for the district council is not necessarily the same officer who dealt with the planning application. Arrange to meet him to discuss the appeal and the basis of the district council's case. See where you agree and where you want to lay more emphasis. When you eventually put forward your views, avoid merely repeating what the planning officer says. That would carry little weight with the inspector. Although you might appear to be on the same side as the district council, do not assume too much. Planning officers might not make all the points you feel are important or place the same emphasis on them. You might however be able to alert the planning officer to some new point that has not been raised previously. Where you get involved in a public inquiry, it is worth coordinating your case with the planning officer's.

Now is a good opportunity to mobilize support by contacting all those who might also have an interest in the planning appeal. See pages 47–52 for some hints on effective tactics.

APPEALS BY WRITTEN REPRESENTATION

The timetable for written representation appeals is generally flexible but try to write before the target date if you can (see

FIGURE 3.2 TIMETABLE FOR AN APPEAL BY WRITTEN REPRESENTATIONS

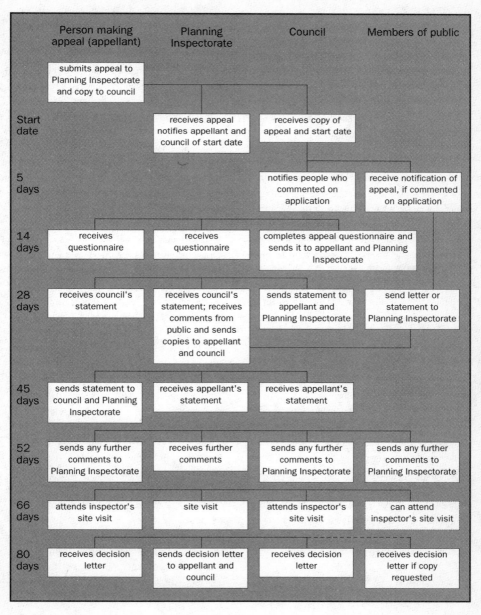

	Person making appeal (appellant)	Planning Inspectorate	Council	Members of public
	submits appeal to Planning Inspectorate and copy to council			
Start date		receives appeal notifies appellant and council of start date	receives copy of appeal and start date	
5 days			notifies people who commented on application	receive notification of appeal, if commented on application
14 days	receives questionnaire	receives questionnaire	completes appeal questionnaire and sends it to appellant and Planning Inspectorate	
28 days	receives council's statement	receives council's statement; receives comments from public and sends copies to appellant and council	sends statement to appellant and Planning Inspectorate	send letter or statement to Planning Inspectorate
45 days	sends statement to council and Planning Inspectorate	receives appellant's statement	receives appellant's statement	
52 days	sends any further comments to Planning Inspectorate	receives further comments	sends any further comments to Planning Inspectorate	sends any further comments to Planning Inspectorate
66 days	attends inspector's site visit	site visit	attends inspector's site visit	can attend inspector's site visit
80 days	receives decision letter	sends decision letter to appellant and council	receives decision letter	receives decision letter if copy requested

Figure 3.2.). Letters received before the inspector's decision is made should be taken into account.

The most important date is the inspector's site inspection, after which he makes a decision. A letter giving the time and date for the inspection is sent to the council and appellant after the appeal is underway and anything you want the inspector to consider must be sent off before this date.

Appeal statements

Your only opportunity to influence the planning inspector in a written representations appeal is by letter or statement. However, any letter you wrote to the council about the planning application will be read by the inspector and, if you have nothing to add, you need not write again.

As with letters of objection to planning applications, it is for you to decide what to say in your appeal statement and how much detail you want to go into, but the general guidelines for writing letters of objection given on pages 40–47 apply even more strictly to letters on appeals – if you want them to be effective.

If you have never seen an appeal planning inspector's decision letter, get hold of one for a similar case from a planning department and read it (see Figure 3.4). Adopt the same sort of format, style and content for your appeal statement. You might find it helpful to structure your appeal statement as follows: introduction; description; background; planning policy; and issues and conclusions.

Introduction

Head the appeal statement with the name of the proposed development, site address, application reference and appeal reference. Then mention anything significant that happened at the application stage that the appellant or council might have ignored. This might be discussions you had with the applicant for example, but avoid 'who said what and when' type descriptions. The inspector is interested in facts, not in arguments between the parties.

State if you represent anyone else – neighbours, residents' association, amenity society or objectors group – what the body you represent is about and how many people you are speaking for.

Description

Inspectors often only have a very short time to study the surrounding area, so set the scene by describing the locality. What you describe depends on the nature of the proposal and how wide its effects would be. Think about both physical appearance and use. For example, with an edge-of-town superstore, you might need to describe: the surrounding countryside because of the visual impact; the road network because of traffic generation; neighbouring houses because of disturbance; and the town centre and other shopping centres in, say, a 16 kilometre (10 mile) radius because of the effects on trade and their prosperity.

If you feel an area has a particular character, try to describe it. This is the sort of detail an inspector might not be able to pick up during a brief inspection. Draw attention to any special features that are relevant – historical associations, ancient buildings, rare wildlife species, or pe-

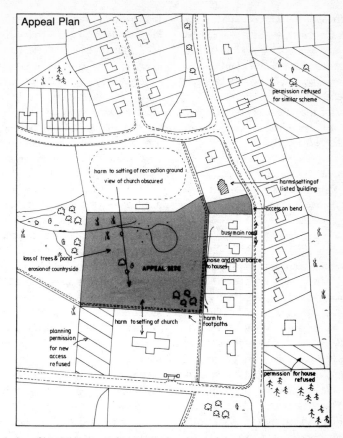

Appeal Plan

harm to setting of recreation ground
view of church obscured

permission refused
for similar scheme

harms setting of
listed building

access on bend

busy main road

loss of trees & pond

erosion of countryside

APPEAL SITE

noise and disturbance
to houses

harm to setting of church

harm to
footpaths

planning
permission
for new
access
refused

permission for house
refused

Appeal plan: Clearly drawn and presented maps and drawings can assist your appeal statements by bringing the planning inspector's attention to particular concerns such as the loss of an amenity.

culiarities of local architecture. The same applies to uses in the area – an old people's home or primary school nearby, a road used by horse riders or parents with children, or the number of takeaways already in the high street.

If you want to take the description of the area farther you could carry out your own surveys. These need not take long to do and, once collected, the information can be included in your text, shown in a table or marked on a map.

Where you are concerned about visual impact:
● travel around the area noting all the places where the site can be seen. Take photographs. Record what is seen

around and near the site, what else the wider view contains, whether it would be screened and what it would be viewed against. Try to establish how many people pass the viewpoint and would see the development;

● judge what the effect of the proposal would be. It is not enough simply to say that it could be seen; and

● consider showing all the viewpoints on a plan. Pictures – photographs and plans – convey a great deal of information and get points across quickly.

Where you are concerned about traffic levels:

● carry out a vehicle count. Find a safe place where you can see the road clearly. Using paper and pen, divide pages into columns, perhaps to show different directions or different kinds of vehicle. Divide pages into rows and record separately half hour, one hour or morning and afternoon time periods. Make a note of the date and time of start and finish; and

● pedestrian and other road user counts can be done in the same way.

Where your concern relates to the loss or overprovision of a use:

● carry out a land use survey. Walk round the vicinity noting down what each building is used for, or just the activities you are interested in. If you are worried about losing housing in a town centre, count the buildings recently converted into offices or shops. If you are concerned about building on green open spaces, see how many are left and where they are, take photographs and compile a detailed list.

Background

In this section of your appeal statement you should set out for the planning inspector any relevant circumstances or history. This can include planning decisions, although these are normally in the council's statement. Where you know, or can find out, the history of a site, include it if relevant, such as where an appellant tries to justify a proposal on the basis of existing levels of activity or the previous existence of buildings. Note any planning applications that have been permitted or refused before, and why. The planning officer's report on the original planning application often provides very useful summaries from which to extract information, so use this information to guide your thinking and arguments in your statement.

Ask the planning officer whether there are any other planning applications and appeals for similar proposals or in similar circumstances that might help you ascertain important issues and how they are dealt with. A company called Compass can search computer records for other appeal decisions on the same type of development, location or issues (see page 148).

Planning policy

In deciding planning applications, planning inspectors place more emphasis on government policy than do district councils. Your appeal statement should take this change in priorities into account, so ask the planning officer what government guidance is applicable to the case. Read through the documents noting anything that relates to the appeal proposal, the title of documents and relevant paragraph numbers to quote in your statement. Then work through the Structure Plan, Local Plan and informal planning policy documents in the same way (see pages 13–17). Again, speak to the planning officer if you need advice on which policies apply. You might find it helpful to look back at what was said about planning policies in letters of objection to planning applications (see page 43–6).

Issues and conclusions

This is the section to express your opinions as persuasively as possible. State what you consider to be the main points, drawing on everything you have looked at, and reach conclusions based on that information. Say what is harmful about the proposed development and why, and what the consequences would be if it were to go ahead as proposed. Conclude your appeal statement by asking to be sent a copy of the inspector's decision letter. When your statement is complete, check that you have the correct address for the Planning Inspectorate (or Inquiry Reporters Unit in Scotland or Planning Appeals Commission in Northern Ireland) and appeal reference. Then take a copy and send off the original.

INSPECTORS' SITE VISITS

The site visit is the planning inspector's opportunity to see the appeal site, surrounding properties and area, and particular points mentioned in letters or statements. No discussion of the merits of the appeal takes place at site visits. In most cases, the appellant, or the appellant's representative, and a planning officer attend the visit, but where a site can be seen clearly from the road or other public land, an inspector is sometimes unaccompanied.

Ask the planning officer to point out any specific physical features of the site, adjoining properties or locality that you feel the inspector should see. If you are not confident that this will be done as you would want, you can ask in your appeal statement to be notified of the inspection so that you can attend – although in most cases this should be unnecessary. About a month after the notice of appeal is submitted, double-check with the planning officer whether the site inspection has been arranged.

INFORMAL HEARINGS

An informal hearing, as the name suggests, is supposed to be a discussion between a planning inspector and the parties in dispute of contentious issues in a planning appeal, and it is on a smaller scale than a public inquiry (see pages 70–4). Appellants can be professionally represented but neither side has the same sort of professional team as at an inquiry. Usually, one or both parties will have asked for the appeal to be dealt with by a public inquiry, but the Planning Inspectorate may offer an informal hearing as an alternative. The district council can confirm whether a hearing is to be held.

An informal hearing takes place after full written statements have been exchanged between the appellant and council. This is supposed to occur within six weeks of the decision to hold an informal hearing or at least three weeks before the hearing date.

You should write with your objections

to the Planning Inspectorate in the same way as you would for a written representations appeal. You will know at this stage which issues will be discussed at the informal hearing. Where all your points can be made adequately in writing, there is nothing to gain by being at the hearing. If you feel you ought to take part, say so in your letter/statement. It is better to attend and say very little than to miss an opportunity. Where a lot of people want to go along, an inquiry is likely to be held instead of an informal hearing.

Look at the appellant's and council's statements at the planning department and write to the Planning Inspectorate if any new points arise. You can attend the hearing regardless of whether you have written a letter, but let the planning officer know that you intend to go along.

At the informal hearing the planning inspector explains the format and ascertains who is present before introducing the appeal, summarizing the cases and outlining the areas he wishes to discuss. The appellant starts the discussion dealing with the issues identified by the inspector. The inspector and district council question the appellant, as may other people present. The same procedure is adopted for the district council to put across its views.

You will be given an opportunity to speak. Although the inspector will want to hear particularly about the issues that he has defined, other points are not totally excluded. The inspector will have your written comments, so do not repeat these points at the informal hearing. The points made on pages 72–4 about speaking at public inquiries are also relevant here. To make an effective contribution, you must

have a full understanding of the parties' cases beforehand, as they will be summarized only briefly by the inspector.

Discussion about the appeal is allowed to continue at the informal hearing site inspection. Thus it differs slightly to site visits for written representations and public inquiries in which those attending are confined to point out only physical features. Again, the inspector will lead the discussion at the site inspection.

PUBLIC INQUIRIES

A public inquiry is a formal hearing of a planning appeal before a member of the Planning Inspectorate, or in Scotland the Inquiry Reporters Unit, or in Northern Ireland the Planning Appeals Commission. It is held in a council's chamber or committee room, village hall or other similar public building and is like a very informal court hearing. A planning inspector presides at the front of the room, the appellant sits on one side and the district council officers opposite. Members of the public, including objectors, usually sit at the back of the room or in a public gallery (see Figure 3.3).

An inquiry can last anything from half a day to a number of months, the length depending on the scale and complexity of the proposal. Between one and three days is common, however. The planning officer will be able to confirm whether there is to be an inquiry and how long it is programmed for. The council should anyway notify you if you objected to the planning application.

Before the inquiry, the council and the person making the appeal (appellant) have to exchange preinquiry statements, which

FIGURE 3.3 A TYPICAL SEATING PLAN AT A PUBLIC INQUIRY AND THE DUTIES OF THOSE INVOLVED

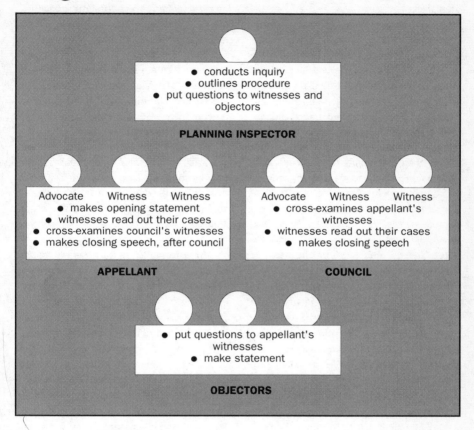

set out the basis of their cases, the sort of evidence they intend to produce and which documents they will refer to. The council's statement should be sent to the appellant six weeks after the appeal is made, the appellant's three weeks after that to the council. Both are available at the planning department, so use the information to help form your own case against the appeal. Note which arguments of the appellant you need to counter, and which areas of your own case require more work.

Where objectors have a comprehensive or complex case and the funds available, a professional or professional team is often employed and the objector is made a 'party' to the appeal. This means he will be more involved in the proceedings and treated similarly to the appellant and council. Like the other parties, a pre-inquiry statement will have to be exchanged. Any professionals employed by objectors must, therefore, have adequate knowledge of inquiry procedure and be suitably qualified.

Three weeks before the inquiry opens, the appellant and council (and objector if party to the inquiry) are supposed to exchange the full cases they intend to make. These are equivalent to their statements in a written representations appeal but usually far more detailed and thorough. Before going to district council offices to look at the statements, you should first check their availability because planning officers are likely to be working on the documents themselves. Make a note of the points you disagree with and any factual errors, recording the page and paragraph number for ease of reference later. These notes will form the basis of your questions to the witnesses. As you work through the cases, think how to frame questions to your best advantage. It is not too late to write again even if you have already sent in your own appeal statement, but comment only on new matters. Alternatively you can deal with any points at the inquiry if you decide to speak, but it is up to each inspector to decide who can participate. Only the appellant, the council, owners/tenants of the land and other planning authorities in the area have the absolute right to take part. In practice, planning inspectors let members of the public speak.

You are not, however, obliged to turn up or speak at the inquiry. You can, if you wish, attend the inquiry but not take part and just observe or just put your objections in writing in exactly the same way as for a written representations appeal (see pages 64–9).

Appellants, councils and objectors can use professional advisers to represent them at inquiries – barristers, solicitors, planning consultants, engineers, landscape architects and others. Any lawyers will act as advocates, leading the professional team. Other members of the team are known as expert witnesses and are 'called' in turn by the advocate to present their 'evidence' (their case) in their respective areas of expertise.

At inquiries, objectors, appellants and councils must be slightly cautious in what they say and do. Each party is expected to bear its own costs of taking part but if someone behaves 'unreasonably' at an inquiry he can become liable for another party's costs.

'Unreasonable' in this sense means recklessly causing another party to incur unnecessary costs at an inquiry. This could be, for example, turning up on the day of an inquiry with a 100 page report on an issue that had not previously been raised, or notified to the appellant in advance. It does not mean merely making a slight mistake or not being familiar with inquiry procedure. Unless you become fully involved in an inquiry, in which case professional help is advisable anyway, the risk of someone claiming costs against you is minimal. Between 1987 and 1992 out of more than 10,000 public inquiries in England, objectors have been liable to pay costs in only a few exceptional cases. If in doubt, speak to a planning officer.

Speaking at public inquiries

Attending and speaking at a public inquiry might seem daunting but it can give your objection more impact. Preparing your case for an inquiry is essentially the same as for a written representations appeal (see pages 64–9). Coordinate your efforts where you can; planning inspectors do not welcome a series of people all making the same point and probably would not allow it. Contact with others at the planning application stage should point you to those likely to attend, and you can discover who else objects by looking at the council's file at the planning department. Decide whether you want to combine your representation at the inquiry or who will make what points.

Arrange a meeting with planning officers to discuss presentation of cases, areas where you can support the council or points that would have more impact coming from you – for example, the existing effect of being next door to a development. If you have special knowledge, the council could call you as one of their witnesses.

Before you go to the inquiry make sure any notes and papers you wish to take along are in good order and that all the points you would like to raise are written down. On the first day of the inquiry, get to the venue in plenty of time, bringing with you all documents or drawings needed for reference. If you want to submit anything new, such as supplementary statements, recent letters or additional plans you have drawn, take three or four extra copies of anything you have not already sent to the Planning Inspectorate. The appellant and district council should have extra copies of their cases to hand out at the inquiry, so ask for a copy if you have not managed to read it beforehand.

When the inquiry opens, indicate when requested by the planning inspector that you want to speak, or that you might do. If you cannot attend the whole inquiry, tell the inspector at this point and he or she will usually arrange a convenient time for you to make your statement. You will be invited to ask questions of each witness at appropriate moments, if you want to do so.

Do take advantage of this opportunity to put questions, as members of the public often ask far more pertinent and awkward questions of witnesses than the professionals. Here are some suggestions for putting questions:

● have a note of your questions in front of you;
● try to order questions by grouping them in subjects or by following the order of the witness's case;
● be ready to summarize the subject area of your questions in case the inspector asks where your line of questioning is leading;
● ask specific questions, do not make statements. You have your chance to do this later;
● do not go over precisely the same ground covered by previous questioners or the inspector will stop you;
● be as concise and brief as possible;
● stick to planning issues; and
● avoid technical points of law and procedure unless you are very confident of your ground.

When the appellant and district council have presented their cases you have your chance to make a statement. As there are no particular formalities to observe, just stand up and state your views simply and clearly. The inspector has to take a note of everything that is said so do not speak so quickly that the gist of your arguments cannot be taken down. He should have a copy of any earlier objection you made in writing so if you have nothing new to add, do not repeat all the same material: just say that you are relying on your written objection, mention anything new that has come up and perhaps summarize in a few sentences two or three main points.

Your statement should be the verbal equivalent of a letter of objection: the reasons why you object, who will be affected and how, and what should be done (see pages 40–7). The difference at an inquiry is that the inspector will stop you (politely) if you waffle or introduce irrelevant facts.

You might need to modify some of the original arguments you had already worked up in the light of what you have heard at the inquiry. Answers to cross-examination questions might have thrown up interesting insights, which you can draw to the inspector's attention.

Be ready to answer questions about your views from the appellant and the inspector. Remember, the appellant might have a barrister skilled at leading witnesses down lines of thought and reasoning helpful to their client's case. This is what they are paid for after all but you should not be asked technical planning questions unless you have gone into such matters in your case. The inspector will intervene if you are asked an unfair question. If you are subject to hostile cross-examination or find a barrister formidable, address your answers to the planning inspector rather than to the questioner. Try not to get flustered: take

your time to think about the question. Ensure your answers are consistent with your main arguments and with each other. If you do not know an answer, say so. If you feel you are not qualified to deal with a particular question, again, say so.

The purpose of inquiries is to test the evidence. Do not rely on assertions that you cannot support or have not thoroughly thought through. If you say a road is very dangerous, get police accident records. If you state a development will be visually damaging, know where you would be able to see it from.

Once all questions have been answered, the council sums up its case in a closing speech. The appellant then makes his closing speech. The inspector then makes arrangements for a formal site inspection and the inquiry closes. Objectors can ask to attend the site inspection, but only do this if it is necessary for you to point out things referred to in your case (see page 69). Check the inspector has a note of all important viewpoints to visit: you can, for example, request the inspector views the site from your property. As with written representations appeals, discussion about the issues and merits of the proposal does not continue at the site inspection.

THE DECISION

Having heard all the evidence and completed his site inspection, the planning inspector writes a decision letter or, if the planning appeal is very large, controversial or legally complex, a report to the Secretary of State.

The length of time between site inspection and decision being issued varies

FIGURE 3.4 A TYPICAL APPEAL DECISION LETTER

Peabody and Co
Archibald House
High Street
Hillton

Your ref: PB/101
Our ref: T/APP/J7593/A/93/347861/K9

25 November 1993

Gentlemen

TOWN AND COUNTRY PLANNING ACT 1990, SECTION 78 AND SCHEDULE 6
APPEAL BY PAINT WARS LIMITED   APPLICATION NO: HA/93/2756

1. I have been appointed by the Secretary of State for the Environment to determine the above appeal. This appeal is against the decision of Hillton District Council to refuse planning permission for the use of land for paintball games and retention of a caravan for use as a changing room. I have considered the written representations made by you and the Council and interested persons. I inspected the site on 25 October 1993.

2. The appeal site is within the Green Hills Area of Outstanding Natural Beauty and comprises some 9 hectares of mixed deciduous native woodland known as Pond Wood. Pond Wood as a whole is an attractive feature in the landscape, and within the wood are a number of important individual trees of great age and character, the subject of Tree Preservation Orders.

3. I consider that the main issues in this case are potential damage to the ecology of the wood, the impact on the wood's visual amenity and impact on adjoining houses.

4. The underlying soil of the wood is clay and I noted on my site visit the significant impact of pedestrian traffic, creating wide muddy paths. In addition to the paths, there are numerous makeshift structures used as cover by participants, in addition to the hut and caravan. These elements are conspicuous, especially when viewed from the public footpath. They significantly detract from the character of the wood, contrary to Structure Plan policies ENV5 and ENV7. There is evidence of damage to trees.

5. I am concerned at the loss of amenity to adjoining houses, especially 'Woodside' which immediately adjoins the access and car park area. Traffic movements immediately adjoining the west flank wall of this dwelling would give rise to significant nuisance. The detailed representations from adjoining residents support my view that residential amenity would be significantly prejudiced were this appeal to be allowed.

6. I have therefore concluded that this appeal should not be allowed, since material harm would be caused to the Area of Outstanding Natural Beauty and to adjoining residents. I have considered all the other matters raised in the representations but I find none of sufficient weight to alter this conclusion.

7. For the above reasons, and in exercise of the powers transferred to me, I hereby dismiss this appeal.

I am Gentlemen
Your obedient Servant

JOHN BRIGHTMAN BA DipTP MRTPI

depending on the complexity of cases; less than three weeks is unusual, four to eight weeks is more common. It can, for a major development proposal, be many months.

Decision letters

The decision letter is sent to whoever made the appeal (that is, the appellant) and the council (see Figure 3.4). You should also receive the decision letter if you asked for a copy in your appeal statement or at the inquiry. Otherwise, you can see the decision letter or buy a copy at the council's planning department.

Appeals are either allowed or dismissed. Allowing or dismissing an appeal amounts to granting or refusing planning permission in the same way that councils decide planning applications. This means that when appeals are allowed, conditions can be attached on design or use. If the application was for outline planning permission, the inspector might make comments about the way the site should be developed, so read the decision letter carefully. What the inspector says beyond the actual decision itself can affect future development proposals. Even if an appeal is allowed, a new planning application can be made for a variation or for something quite different.

When you have read the decision letter, discuss any implications and points that you do not understand with the planning officer.

Appeals are sometimes dismissed for reasons that the appellant can overcome: for example, an inspector might say that a site is suitable for development but the actual scheme put forward was not the right one. A dismissed appeal is not therefore necessarily the end of the line. Any future planning applications will be judged against what the inspector says in his decision letter. If a planning application is made for the same development on the same site within two years, in the absence of a change in circumstances the council can refuse to process it. This stops applicants trying to wear down councils and objectors by making repetitive planning applications. Apart from this, there is nothing to stop new applications being made.

CHALLENGING APPEAL DECISIONS

Appeal decisions can be challenged in the courts within six weeks of the decision letter being issued. Decisions can only be challenged on legal grounds – that the inspector acted outside his authority or prejudice was caused by a failure to follow correct procedure. Decisions cannot be challenged on their planning merits or matters of opinion.

In England in 1991/92, out of more than 20,000 appeal decisions 139 were challenged: eighty-nine by appellants, forty-four by councils and six by others. During the same year, 101 challenges were decided by the courts and less than half the inspectors' appeal decisions were overturned. Of the twenty-eight appeals re-decided, the original decision was confirmed in fifteen cases.

In most instances, leave the job of challenging appeal decisions to the council. Consult a solicitor experienced in planning work before thinking about taking such a step yourself: you would need to have funds running into many thousands of pounds to take an appeal decision to court.

COMPLAINTS

If you feel there was something wrong with procedure at an inquiry, you can complain to the Council on Tribunals and if you are unhappy with how you were treated by the inspector, you can write to the Chief Planning Inspector at the Planning Inspectorate. In Scotland, approach the Principal Clerk at the Scottish Office Inquiry Reporters Unit and in Northern Ireland the Chief Commissioner at the Planning Appeals Commission.

The Ombudsman deals with unfair treatment through maladministration including failure to follow proper procedures.

Complaints about district councils are researched by the Local Government Ombudsman (see page 56) and those about central government departments including the Department of the Environment, Scottish Office, Welsh Office and Northern Ireland DoE are investigated by the Parliamentary Ombudsman, but only at the request of a Member of Parliament. The Ombudsman has booklets about investigations so read these before deciding whether to make a complaint. The addresses of these bodies appear on page 145.

Note that none of the above can question the merit of an appeal decision or change the result.

APPEALS – ACTION CHECK LIST

1 Check with the district council whether a planning appeal has been made.

2 Find out the date for submitting comments and the date of the inquiry or informal hearing (if there is going to be one).

3 Study the appeal documents and make notes.

4 Contact the planning officer to discuss the appeal and stay in touch to monitor progress.

5 Alert other potential objectors and the media.

6 Write your appeal statement and send it to the Planning Inspectorate, in Scotland to the Inquiry Reporters Unit or in Northern Ireland to the Planning Appeals Commission. Ask to receive a copy of the decision letter.

7 Read the statements by the council and the person making the appeal at the district council and write a further letter if new points arise.

8 Where a public inquiry/informal hearing is to be held, prepare your case and attend.

9 Look at planning inspector's decision letter.

Chapter 4

DEVELOPMENT WITHOUT PLANNING PERMISSION

We know that most development should have planning permission before being carried out – but what happens if it does not? This is one of the most vexed questions in the whole planning system. Members of the general public have an important role to play in spotting and alerting councils to unauthorized development. We therefore now look at what you can realistically do when you think development is taking place without permission or is breaking the conditions of planning permission.

Nearby occupiers are often affected by an activity such as vehicles arriving and leaving, lorries using an unsuitable access or visually damaging activity in the landscape. Alternatively, building work might start where you would not expect to see it – in open countryside, close to your boundary or on a Listed Building. When you see something like this happening, you will not know whether it is authorized or not.

WHAT YOU CAN DO

The first thing to do is to get your facts straight, so telephone or visit the planning department and ask whether planning permission has been given or look up the planning record to see what planning permissions there might be. Even where permission exists, the development can still be breaking conditions or not being carried out as approved.

If a planning application has been made, but not decided, follow the advice set out in Chapter 2. Where no planning permission exists and no application has been made, there are a number of steps you can take, but do not put off action for too long. There are time limits on councils to take action (see page 83).

Apart from using the planning system, you might be able to take legal action yourself, depending on the circumstances. This could be where trespass is taking place, there is damage to your property, where statutory nuisance arises or a covenant in title deeds is breached. Speak to your Citizens Advice Bureau or solicitor about this.

Crowdale District Council Planning Record Card
LAND SOUTH OF HOME FARM, CHURCH LANE

Ref no.	Description	Decision	Appeal
126/62	Use of land as caravan site	Granted 1/7/63	
485/65	Erection of office/toilets	Granted 4/11/65	
87/75	Extension for indoor sports area	Granted 9/3/75	
983/79	Outline, 15 houses	Refused 12/2/80	Dismissed 8/2/81
412/81	Change of use to farm shop	Granted 20/10/81	
756/87	Change of use to light industrial units	Refused 3/6/87	Allowed 2/3/88
1107/92	Erection of two new light industrial units	Granted 9/9/92	

A record of all planning applications and decisions made on a property is kept by the district council. Often there is a record card or sheet for each property.

If someone has carried out building work, is using a property or intends to carry out development, it is possible he or she has applied to the district council for a Lawful Development Certificate to establish whether the development is allowable without planning permission. This certificate states whether or not planning permission is legally needed for a development; it does not consider the planning merits of the development: for example, an application was made at Walton-on-Thames, Surrey to ascertain whether a tennis court with an underground triple garage below required a planning application. The council thought it did but, on appeal, the Secretary of State decided the proposal came within permitted development rules and, therefore, no application was needed.

You could see an application for a Lawful Development Certificate advertised in the local paper or receive notification through the post. Councils do not have to publicize these applications but often do as the history and existing use of a property is sometimes crucial to the council's decision. Evidence from local people can therefore be especially important.

Contacting the developer

Apart from Lawful Development Certificates, there is usually no planning application when unauthorized development is being investigated so we use the term 'developer' here in place of 'applicant'. Developers could be private individuals, small businesses, site operators, farmers or builders.

When you suspect unauthorized development is occurring, you could try discussing the development with the person responsible but discretion is needed. The type of person who ignores or flouts planning regulations, often where significant profit is at stake, is not likely to give a warm welcome to outside interest. Better to go through official channels than to sour a relationship with a neighbour or get into an argument.

Developers might be unaware that planning permission is needed but most probably they are taking a chance, hoping no one notices. If they know you are aware of what they are doing and that you are prepared to take it farther, they might stop or be persuaded to make a planning application.

Through friendly discussion you might be able to discover precisely what is going on and whether there is in fact unauthorized development at all. Discussion might result in activity being changed in a way that would make it acceptable to you. So much the better if this can be achieved without the need for an official complaint.

Meeting the planning officer

If a development still concerns you, contact the planning department, which will point you to the officer you need to speak to initially. Tell him or her what activity is going on, when it started, who is doing it, where it is taking place, and why you are concerned. Ask the officer to investigate.

Some district councils do not take action, except in more extreme cases, unless they receive a complaint, so you might be asked to put your complaint in writing. This will be kept confidential by the district council. The letter of complaint does not have to be a comprehensive statement:

just set out briefly the facts you told the officer initially.

Following a complaint, officers look up the planning history and any planning permissions that exist. They will visit the property and speak to the owner or occupier, and possibly to neighbours. Councils can serve notices on owners and occupiers to get more information about what is going on. The officers are then in a position to form a view on whether there is unauthorized development.

Contacting councillors

Where nothing happens after your initial complaint or there are long periods when no action seems to be taken, first establish with the planning department that the development you are concerned about is actually unauthorized and one that the council can potentially do something about. Then think about lobbying councillors. Your approach should be similar to that advised when seeking the support of councillors in opposing a planning application (see pages 39–40).

Development taking place without planning permission undermines councillors' powers of development control, and they are often as concerned about this aspect as they are about the effects of the development itself. Tell the councillor what has happened, what you have done about it so far and ask him to look into the case. In most instances a councillor will ask an officer to investigate or for information about the case. Invite the councillor to visit the site with you so he can see the effects of the unauthorized development – disturbance, traffic, appearance or whatever. Failing this send him photographs.

Unlike planning applications, where councils have to react to proposals, the onus here is on councils to initiate action. With competing pressures on officers, a bit of lobbying and a councillor's strong support can get that action taken or move the problem up the list of priorities.

Usually, a report on the unauthorized development will go to a planning committee, so check with the planning department if it is and when. This can be a good point to urge a councillor to press for immediate action. You can attend the planning committee meeting but let the councillor you have lobbied know that you are going to attend.

Seeking support

If you are concerned by an activity going on without planning permission, so then are others likely to be. As with planning applications, there is strength in numbers: the more people who complain and the louder they do so, the greater the likelihood that the council will act. Mobilize support by alerting other people and advising them what to do (see pages 47–52).

Where the unauthorized development is small scale, it could affect only those in the immediate area. Even here, however, it might set a precedent which, if unchallenged, others could follow. This could then give it added significance. Where the history of the property is important, contacting other objectors might put you in touch with someone who knows about it in detail, which could be useful for your case and for the council's.

Contact the parish council, which will probably be concerned at the infringement of planning control, in addition to the development itself. Encourage parish councillors to contact the district council complaining about the unauthorized development and urging prompt action.

WHAT COUNCILS CAN DO

Most councils have enforcement officers who investigate unauthorized development and complaints. They are not necessarily qualified planning officers but do have the support of the planning department behind them. An enforcement officer's role is often to collect information, which planning officers then weigh up and act upon.

Enforcement action

The various powers that councils possess to take action against unauthorized development are known collectively as enforcement. Enforcement is a controversial and difficult area, the subject of a

great deal of litigation. The number of cases where formal action is taken by councils in England is estimated at around 15,000 a year. Here are some examples where action was taken:

● car boot sales taking place in the Green Belt at Averley, Essex;

● a 3.3 metre (11 foot) deep hole dug in a garden at Hampstead Heath, London; and

● double glazing units put in a listed Queen Anne farmhouse at Downley, Buckinghamshire.

Some uses seem prone to going ahead without planning permission – car breakers and scrap yards, waste disposal and transfer, and car repair and spraying. Often they are uses that are both very profitable and unpleasant to live near. In some instances there is no doubt that development is carried out flagrantly, with blatant disregard for planning controls. In others,

In this typical example of unauthorized development, poultry sheds and their surroundings were transformed into a builder's yard and car crash repair works in which panel beating and paint spraying took place. Fifteen years after the uses began, the council has failed to stop the unauthorized development; appeals on this case went all the way to the House of Lords.

considering the complexity of some planning law and grey areas of interpretation, it can happen quite innocently. Development that is not carried out exactly as approved in a planning permission or fails to comply with conditions on a planning permission can also be the subject of enforcement action.

It is not a criminal offence to carry out development without planning permission, but where a council takes action and the offender does not comply then he can be prosecuted. Fines of up to £20,000 can be imposed. However, work on Listed Buildings, Scheduled Ancient Monuments, Tree Preservation Order trees and demolition in Conservation Areas without the appropriate permission is a criminal offence.

Members of the public cannot take enforcement action themselves or insist that a district council does on their behalf, because district councils have discretion on whether to act. Since this can be the cause of great frustration and bitterness to the public, we shall look at the reasons why councils do not or cannot take enforcement action:

● the activity taking place might not come within the meaning of development for planning purposes (see pages 11–13).
● planning permission could have been granted by the council, or at appeal. Applicants usually have up to five years to carry out development and a planning permission, perhaps contentious when first approved, could have been renewed several times. If all conditions requiring approval of details, materials and landscaping are complied with, and the scheme goes ahead in line with the approved plans, there is little a council can do short of revoking planning permissions. This is a drastic step that can be very expensive as compensation is paid to the owner by the council;
● development could be of a type allowed under the 'permitted development' rules in which the government in effect grants automatic planning permission for many types of building work and uses: everything from building a garage to holding stock car race meetings (see pages 14–15). In certain circumstances councils can take away these automatic rights (see Chapter 7) or approve only certain aspects of the development. More normally, however, the 'permitted development' can just go ahead without anyone being notified;
● aside from changes that come within the 'permitted development' regime, other changes of use are allowed without planning permission by the government under its 'use classes order' (see page 16). Thus, no permission is needed for a building society to become a betting shop or a church an art gallery;
● there are time limits for taking enforcement action, so, if nothing is done within the specified times, councils cannot take action afterwards. Such development is then said to be 'immune from enforcement'. The time limits are four years for building works and using any building to live in and ten years for changes of use and breaking planning conditions; and
● finally, as a matter of policy the government discourages enforcement action just because development is unauthorized. When planning rules are infringed, councils are supposed to act only in situations

where they would not grant planning permission, or not without conditions. Even if a council does not itself like a development, it must take into account whether it would be given permission at appeal. If it would, the council is unlikely to take action.

These then are the legitimate planning reasons why councils might not do anything about unauthorized development. There could, of course, be other non-planning reasons (see page 17).

When you make a complaint to the council, the planning officers should let you know the outcome of these investigations. If they conclude there is nothing the council can do, they should explain why. If you are not satisfied with their response, think about getting separate professional advice for confirmation.

Enforcement procedure

Where an unauthorized development is harmful, planning or enforcement officers can contact developers and try to persuade them either to stop what they are doing or to make a planning application. If the developer does neither, the planning officer writes a report, which is put on an agenda for a planning committee meeting. Sometimes reports on delicate enforcement cases and discussion about them are not made public. The planning committee decides whether to authorize officers to take enforcement action. Often, a committee delays taking such a decision until all other avenues are exhausted and meanwhile asks officers to negotiate with the developer. Beyond staying in touch with the officers to keep abreast of events,

there is little you can do within the enforcement procedures at this stage.

In most cases, an enforcement notice is served on the owner and occupier requiring the activity to cease, the land to be returned to its former condition, buildings to be demolished or some other remedy (see Figure 4.1). The notice says how long the council gives the developer to carry out what he or she has been required to do. A council can, however, only take action against that part or aspect of the development that infringes planning rules: for example, a horticultural business at Tarleton, Lancashire was selling produce grown both on site and bought in from elsewhere. Agricultural businesses are allowed to sell their own produce, so enforcement action taken by West Lancashire District Council was only against the sale of items bought in for resale.

If a council also serves a stop notice, the unauthorized activity must cease straightaway. These are used very rarely as compensation can be claimed by the developer if a council gets its facts wrong or makes mistakes in procedure.

A person who receives an enforcement notice can appeal against it, comply with it, or ignore it. The last course is likely to land him in court. Prosecution is something only the council can do. If the developer complies, that should be the end of the matter as the notice continues to have effect. A watchful eye might be needed to check that activity does not recur in the future. If it does, contact the planning department again and tell them what is happening. You could take photos to support your contentions.

A developer who does not comply with

FIGURE 4.1 A COUNCIL'S POWERS OF ENFORCE-MENT AGAINST UNAUTHORIZED DEVELOPMENT

Planning Contravention Notice
Used to find out what is happening at properties where there might be unauthorized development. Served on owners, occupiers and operators, with twenty-one days to respond. Notice asks about: types of activities going on; when they began; names and addresses of owners, occupiers and operators; any existing planning permissions; and any reasons why planning permission is not needed.

Enforcement Notice
Used to stop or remedy unauthorized development that has already taken place. Served on owners, occupiers and anyone else affected. States the unauthorized development, what must be done about it, and in what time. Comes into effect after twenty-eight days, unless appeal made to Secretary of State.

Stop Notice
Used only with enforcement notice. Stops unauthorized development before enforcement notice comes into effect or while an appeal is running. Councils liable to pay compensation for loss or damage caused if notice withdrawn or mistakes over facts or procedure made. Used where a developer knew planning permission was needed, refuses to make planning application, and is causing severe harm.

Breach of Condition Notice
Used where condition on planning permission that is carried out is not complied with. States what conditions are concerned, what must be done to comply, and within what period. No appeal to Secretary of State; can only be challenged in magistrates court.

Injunctions
Used where serious and irreversible harm would be caused. Issued by High Court or county courts using their discretionary powers. Stops unauthorized activity starting or continuing.

'Section 215' Notice
Used to get untidy land and buildings cleaned up. Does not apply to untidiness caused in ordinary course of lawful activity. Served on owners and occupiers. Sets out what steps must be taken and gives time limit of at least twenty-eight days. No appeal to Secretary of State, can only be challenged in magistrates court.

an enforcement notice can be prosecuted, but going to court is expensive and time consuming so a council is inevitably reluctant to take this step. It might therefore be months before the council takes formal action, especially where unauthorized development does not threaten life, limb and public safety.

APPEALS AGAINST ENFORCEMENT

In England and Wales about 7,000 enforcement appeals are made every year; over one-third of these are later withdrawn. Of those decided at appeal, almost two-thirds are dismissed, less than one-third are allowed, and in the remainder of cases the enforcement notice is only partially successful.

The various specified grounds for appealing against enforcement notices include that the development does not need planning permission, the alleged activity is not taking place and that planning permission for the development ought to be granted anyway. The issues disputed in an enforcement appeal can be about facts, legal opinion and planning merits.

An appeal against an enforcement notice is, in practice, similar to an appeal when planning permission has been refused. Like a planning appeal it can be decided by written representations, informal hearing or public inquiry (see pages 64–74). You have all the same opportunities to influence the decision. The most effective way to deal with an appeal is described in Chapter 3.

Where an appeal against an enforcement notice is made, the unauthorized development can continue. There might,

however, be practical reasons why a developer would not carry on, such as the possibility of having to demolish or restore buildings, but only the council serving a stop notice or getting a court injunction can bring an unauthorized development to an immediate halt.

An applicant can also appeal if he disagrees with a council's decision on an application for a Lawful Development Certificate. The basis for these appeals is only that planning permission is not needed, and here the arguments are about fact and the law, but not about planning merits.

Enforcement appeal statements

For both enforcement and Lawful Development Certificate appeals, confirm with the planning officer what issues are going to be relevant. This depends on the precise nature of the application and on the grounds on which the developer appeals. At the same time find out what the council are going to do themselves and ask whether there is any information the officer thinks you could usefully provide to help the council with its case. Make sure what you propose to do is going to be relevant to the decision. If you know about the property – possibly because you live or work nearby – the officer might ask whether you would be prepared to give evidence if an inquiry is being held. Also check the time scale for submitting your comments and confirm the application reference and address to send comments to.

Look back to pages 66–9 for guidance on drawing up an appeal statement to send to the Planning Inspectorate. For both enforcement and Lawful Development Certificate appeals concentrate on factual evidence to show why the development is harmful. Contrast the situation before with the situation afterwards. You can collect valuable information about an unauthorized use by observing the site (see pages 66–8). If you decide to do this, think very carefully about your personal safety; do not put yourself in danger. Planning officers sometimes have police escorts when serving enforcement notices and going on to sites.

In your enforcement appeal statement, include a request to receive a copy of the decision letter. Once your statement is complete, copy it and send the original to the Planning Inspectorate, remembering to show the appeal reference clearly. If a public inquiry or informal hearing is to be held, follow the steps set out on pages 69–74.

THE DECISION

An enforcement decision letter is similar to one for a planning appeal. Depending on the circumstances, the planning inspector or Secretary of State decides:

- planning permission is not needed;
- an enforcement notice is not valid;
- planning permission is needed but is granted; or
- planning permission is needed and is refused.

Where enforcement action is upheld on appeal, the decision letter can vary the amount of time given to remedy the unauthorized development. When an enforcement notice comes into effect after an appeal, the situation is as described on pages 84–6.

If a council does not act properly or effectively in dealing with a case of development without planning permission, you can complain to the Local Government Ombudsman (see page 56).

UNAUTHORIZED DEVELOPMENT – ACTION CHECK LIST

1 Check with the district council whether planning permission is needed.
2 Speak to a planning or enforcement officer about unauthorized development.
3 Contact the developer.
4 Contact the parish and district councillors.
5 Alert other potential objectors and the media.
6 Write a letter of complaint to the district council.
7 Monitor the council's action and progress.
8 If there is an appeal, write an enforcement appeal letter or statement and send it to the Planning Inspectorate, Inquiry Reporters Unit or Planning Appeals Commission.
9 Where an inquiry is held, prepare for it and attend.
10 Look at the planning inspector's decision letter.
11 Check the unauthorized development does not recur.

Chapter 5

LOCAL PLANS

Local Plans are the district council's blueprint for the future of your village, town, city and area. The policies that they contain touch your life every day. If you want a say in the future of your environment and community, you need to get involved in the Local Plan-making process. Your actions at this stage can be more effective than trying to stop or influence planning permission later, because planning applications and appeals are decided by reference to Local Plans. By influencing the content of these Plans, you can help set the criteria for planning decisions.

Development for most of the United Kingdom into the next century will be settled over the next few years, because new laws put in place in 1991 mean that all districts are expected to have a Local Plan covering the whole of their area by 1996. There is therefore going to be Local Plan preparation on a massive scale as never seen before. It is up to you to make your views known and to look after your interests; do not assume that councils will do this for you. Developers and landowners are becoming increasingly involved in Local Plan preparation: so should you.

The government estimates that only 20 per cent of the population of England and Wales were covered by statutory Local Plans in 1992. Out of 333 non-metropolitan districts, seventy did not have any Local Plans and only fifty-four had a Plan covering the whole district. In Scotland, by 1992 there were about 220 adopted Local Plans and just over 100 being drawn up or reviewed. More than half the districts had a Plan covering the whole of their area in place or under preparation. By the end of 1992, all but three of the twenty-six districts in Northern Ireland had an adopted Local Plan.

In theory, Local Plans are supposed to cater for a ten-year period and should be reviewed every five years, but, in practice, they are reviewed at irregular intervals, depending on pressures for change and the available resources of the district council. Typical chapter headings and content of a Local Plan are shown in Figure 5.1.

GETTING INVOLVED

Bearing in mind their fundamental importance to everyone living, working or owning property in an area, it is surprising how few people are aware of the existence of Local Plans. Although district councils publish notices in local papers, issue press releases, hold exhibitions and display information at the planning department, it is easy to miss publicity about Local Plans.

Your parish council and local conservation and amenity groups as well as other local groups who might be interested are informed about the plans being drawn up. If you are part of a group who want to comment on a Local Plan, register your interest with the council.

The best bet, if you do not want to miss the opportunity to influence the policies that affect you and your community, is to contact the Local Plan section of the planning department at your district council. Ask whether there is an adopted Plan or whether one is being prepared and what stage it has reached. Make sure you fully understand the answer as the Local Plan process is complicated. There may be more than one Local Plan covering the district and these could be at different stages in the process.

If there are one or two issues or particular sites you are interested in, mention them and ask how they are affected by Local Plan preparation. Arrange to meet a planning officer if you are in any doubt. Where you are concerned about the possibility of mining, quarrying or waste disposal, contact the county council for information about the relevant Plans.

The Local Plans officer should be able to indicate when a Plan that is being prepared is likely to be published for public comment. Ask him to notify you when a

FIGURE 5.1 TOPICS COVERED BY A LOCAL PLAN

Introduction
Plan preparation
Relationship with other plans
Plan purpose and objectives
Monitoring and review of plan

Housing
Policy context
Amount and location of new housing
Housing needs
Conversions and changes of use
Special needs
Design and environment

Employment
Assessment of need
Amount and location of office and
    industrial development
Business areas
Commercial development in the
    countryside
Small businesses
Relocating badly sited industry

Shopping
Existing shopping centres
Amount, type and location of shopping
    development
Local and neighbourhood shops
Maintaining town centres
Retail warehouses and superstores
Access for disabled

Built environment and conservation
New development and redevelopment
Extensions and alterations
Trees and open space
Shop fronts and advertisements
Conservation Areas

Listed Buildings
Protecting archaeological remains

Countryside
Development restraint outside built-up
    areas
Development in Green Belts and Areas
    of Outstanding Natural Beauty
Landscape improvement
Rural housing and employment
Agriculture and agricultural buildings
Nature conservation and Sites of
    Special Scientific Interest

Highways and transportation
New roads
Road improvements
Parking standards
Town centre traffic management
Facilities for public transport
Highways and new development

Recreation, tourism and leisure
Provision of sport and leisure facilities
Uses in the countryside
Holiday accommodation
Tourist attractions
Playing fields
Country parks
Amusement arcades

Utilities and community services
Public utilities – gas, water, electricity,
    drainage, post office
    telecommunications
Schools and education
Health facilities
Community facilities
Libraries

Plan reaches a stage where you can comment. For your contribution to have maximum impact, it is essential that you find out the dates for submitting your comments and objections as early as possible. Meanwhile, stay in touch with the planning department to keep abreast of progress. Alternatively, if you think you might eventually get professional help, get a planning consultant to monitor Local Plan progress for you.

When councils have worked up a first draft Local Plan, it is approved by the planning committee for publication. A Plan at this stage is often called a 'consultation draft'. This the council publicizes to get public reaction and invites consultees to make representations about the Plan. There is no set period for this stage, although it is usually at least six weeks.

Councils consider feedback and a revised plan, drawn up by planning officers, is approved by councillors. A district council applies to the respective county council for a certificate stating that the draft Plan conforms with the county's Structure Plan. The Plan is then published as a 'deposit draft'.

In this slightly more formal stage in the procedure, a Plan is put on deposit for at least six weeks, during which anyone can make formal comments. Again, councils take steps to involve the public and get reactions from consultees. A statement about publicity, public participation and consultation is also available from the council.

Comments on the deposit draft are classified as objections, which are against some aspect of the Plan, or representations, which support some aspect of the Plan. We will generally refer to both as 'objections' in this chapter as the same considerations apply.

Studying a Local Plan

Once you ascertain that a Local Plan has been published, track down a copy at the district council office, parish council office or local libraries, or buy one from the district council.

Read the introduction and summary, if there is one, to help set the scene for you. Next, look at the index. Assuming you do not want to read the whole Plan cover to cover, turn to the issues that interest you and read those sections. There is often some overlap so do go through the index carefully to avoid missing something important.

Look at the proposals map, together with its key, to get an overview of the main land classifications. If it is a particular area or site you are concerned about, find it on the proposals map or inset map and see if it is allocated for a use or designated in some way. Make a note and look up relevant policies in the written part of the Plan.

Where you are worried about certain types of development, or even specific development proposals, see how the policies of the Plan affect them. There could be loopholes to close or new policies to suggest, to stop that development in future.

Study how the plan deals with issues that concern you: policies might be weak, inappropriate or there might not be a policy dealing with a particular point. You can object to a Plan on the basis that it omits policies that ought to be in there.

LOCAL PLAN INSET MAP

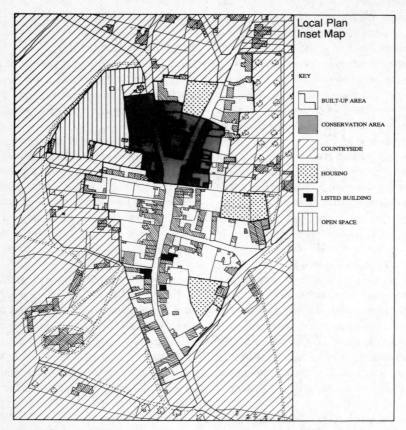

**Local Plan
Inset Map**

KEY

BUILT-UP AREA

CONSERVATION AREA

COUNTRYSIDE

HOUSING

LISTED BUILDING

OPEN SPACE

Local Plans are often very confusing, especially if you have never seen one before. Do not let this worry you or put you off. Local Plans are easier to understand if you make full use of the fully annotated proposals maps and inset maps included in each Plan.

As you study the Plan, write down points that occur to you as well as policy and paragraph numbers for future reference. If you do not understand any part of the Plan, ask to speak to a planning officer. He is usually helpful and will clarify uncertainties for you.

Meeting the planning officer

Although there are specific periods in the Local Plan process for making representations and formal objections, there is nothing to stop you discussing the Plan with a planning officer at any time. Even where a Plan has been finalized recently, suggestions should be noted by the district council and taken into account later. In many ways it is a good idea to get in an early comment to sow the seeds for the future. The farther the Plan is advanced, the more entrenched the officer's views are likely to be. Because the Plan cannot actually be altered until it is formally reviewed, this may also affect the degree of interest shown by the officer (see page 100).

When a Local Plan is published you can arrange to meet a planning officer or speak on the telephone. Mention your concerns and how you feel the Plan might be improved, using your notes to back up your arguments. Listen carefully to the district council's views and the thinking behind the policies, but do not be put off about points that you feel strongly about, without good reason. A draft Plan contains the policies that the planning officers think are right for the area; naturally, they have a tendency to defend them. Use the information you get from the planning officer to refine your views on the Plan.

Do not withdraw your objection unless you have firm guarantees that the Plan will be amended. It is better to maintain your objection and explain what agreement has been reached in your objection form or statement than risk losing out and not achieving any results.

Once you are involved in the Plan, you should be told of any modifications relevant to your objections, or you can get in touch with the officers periodically to keep up to date. Lists of proposed modifications can be inspected at the planning department.

Lobbying councillors

Ultimately, it is the elected council members who decide what goes in the Local Plan, and so it is they who must be influenced. Councillors set the tenor of the Plan and what issues it must address, while the planning officers carry out the technical side of Plan preparation.

Councils often set up sub committees or working parties to oversee Local Plans. Find out the names of the relevant councillors from the planning department. Before approaching a councillor, bear in mind the main stages at which he has to make decisions (see Figure 5.2):

- forming initial ideas;
- approving a consultation draft;
- considering comments and approving a revised deposit draft;
- reacting to objections;
- considering the Local Plan inquiry inspector's report and planning officers' suggested modifications to it; and
- adopting the Plan.

These are all opportunities for lobbying councillors to influence the Local Plan. For general comments on contacting councillors refer to pages 39–40.

As with planning officers, it can be very worthwhile approaching councillors as early as possible – before anything is published – as the council is supposed to reflect the demands of people in the area. If there are particular issues such as types of development, areas that need protecting and traffic problems that you feel something should be done about, draw these to a councillor's attention. Write or meet him at a routine weekly surgery or ask him to attend a meeting of your group.

FIGURE 5.2 PREPARING A LOCAL PLAN

Stages of preparation	Opportunities for action by general public
Draft Plan District council draws up draft proposal and planning policies	Discuss your concerns and views on development with councillors and planning officers
Consultation Draft Plan published, sent to official consultees and publicized in the area	Submit comments to council and lobby councillors
Plan revised Comments and representations considered, Plan altered and approved by councillors	
Deposit and objections Deposit Plan published and publicized, objections and supporting representations submitted in minimum 6 week deposit period	Submit objection/ representation form and lobby councillors
Negotiation and modifications Planning officers try to overcome objections and put forward modifications to the Plan	Discuss objection with planning officers
Local Plan inquiry Inspector hears council's and objectors' cases	Draw up statement and/or speak at the inquiry
Inspector's report Report sent to council, which decides what changes to make	Lobby councillors
Modifications and objections Inspector's report and council's proposed modifications to the Plan published, objections submitted in minimum 6 week period, council considers objections	Submit fresh objection/modification
Further inquiry If necessary, inspector hears objections to modifications and reports to council	Draw up fresh statement and/or speak at the inquiry
Plan adopted Council publicizes intention to adopt Plan formally and after 28 days votes to adopt, when it becomes a statutory plan	

Councillors can themselves be objectors to the Local Plan: they might object to part of the Plan that affects their own area. They can also agree to represent residents or interested groups at a Local Plan inquiry: for example, at the Nuneaton and Bedworth Borough Plan inquiry, individual objectors to a 52 hectare (128 acre) housing site had difficulty in coordinating their action so a councillor helped by acting as their advocate. Drawing up Local Plans takes years and council elections will occur during this period, so use these as an opportunity to secure councillors' support for your ideas.

Lobbying consultees

When Local Plans are made available for public inspection, they are also sent to a wide variety of national and local organizations for comment. Only when the Local Plan is put on deposit – that is awaiting formal reactions as opposed to the informal ones at earlier stages in Local Plan preparation – does the council issue a list of who was consulted. Check the list to make sure that all groups or bodies you think might be interested were consulted and take their address to contact as potential supporters.

In most cases, it is not appropriate to approach what we might call technical consultees, such as government advisory bodies and public utilities. However, if your concerns relate specifically to one or more of these bodies, you can contact them direct. Find out the appropriate department in the organization, discuss your concern and see what they say. Their response could change your tack slightly or back up your arguments when you put your case

forward. Speaking to a consultee could also possibly result in him looking at the Plan again in the light of your particular concern.

Other objectors

So far, when we have talked about other objectors we mean other people who, like you, oppose a development. With Local Plans the situation is more complex: other objectors fall into two camps – those who share your views and those who want to change a Plan in a way that you feel will be harmful.

Just as you might object to aspects of a Local Plan, so developers and landowners certainly will, but their objectives will be to get land they own allocated for development, to remove or modify policies that restrict development and to secure new road links or other facilities that would be to their advantage. This sort of Local Plan objector is the equivalent of the applicant, appellant or developer in previous chapters.

We look first at getting support from people who share your views about a Plan.

Getting support

Similar considerations apply to objecting to a Local Plan as to objecting to a planning application. The more people who object to a particular policy or land allocated for development, the greater the chance notice will be taken. To mobilize support for your objection do all the things that are set out on pages 47–52.

Formal objections, made at the deposit stage, are available for the public to see, but comments made on the earlier consultation draft are not. Check with the district council planning department whether anyone else objects to the same policies as you. Try contacting them to talk about the issues. See whether there is common ground and discuss taking action together. Their names and addresses will be on the formal objection forms.

When trying to enlist support from neighbours, local traders, businesses or whoever, do not expect them to know about the Plan or its contents. You will probably have some educating to do. Your main objectives here are to get people to write to the council when the consultation draft is published and to object to the Plan when it goes on deposit. Make sure people know the dates for submitting their comments. In any publicity material explain why the Plan is important and which aspects of it are unsatisfactory.

The Local Plan process is long and tedious for all but the truly dedicated. Objection fatigue can set in. If others, or indeed you, are not able to do anything else, just concentrate on the two main objectives: write a letter or complete a form at the consultation stage; and complete a form at the deposit stage.

The benefit of Local Plan preparation being a drawnout business is that you do have time to organize support for your objection. Where there is sufficient support to form an action group or committee, you can launch a concerted campaign and possibly raise money to fund professional representation at the public inquiry. Alternatively, you can represent other objectors yourself, which means your written statement and speaking at the inquiry can be done on behalf of many people. Otherwise, decide in advance who is going

to deal with which issue – effect of traffic, impact on landscape, effect on your properties and so on. The inspector is unlikely to let a string of objectors stand up and make exactly the same points, or to ask the planning officers similar questions. Good planning arguments are what the inspector is looking for, not weight of numbers.

We look now at the other sort of Local Plan objector – ones who want to change a Plan in a way that you do not agree with.

Adverse objections

Countering objections that you do not agree with can be difficult and technically complicated because, in theory, it is not possible to object to another objection. The district council draws up its Plan, the public, including developers, can object to it. The objector and the council argue on the merits of the Plan and the objection, and the Local Plan inspector makes recommendations on those relative merits. An objection, therefore, is not like a planning application or appeal on which the views of the public are sought.

In practice, a representation in support of the relevant draft Local Plan policy is made to counter someone else's undesirable objection. If an objection throws up some new point or issue, you can object to the Plan on the basis that it should include a policy on that matter. Making an objection puts you in a stronger position at the inquiry because objectors have the right to speak.

Countering adverse objections can also be tricky because you probably will not know what objections are made until the Plan reaches the deposit stage. Even then, unless you check what is submitted during the six-week objection period, you will not find out about objections made by others. It is easy to miss a controversial proposal put forward by a developer or other body. A common tactic used by developers is to submit objections right at the end of the deposit period for this reason.

The best that can be done is to check with the planning officer as often as you reasonably can. As there will be hundreds of objections, the officer might not be able to help unless it is something very specific you are concerned about, like one piece of land. Therefore, if you can, go to the planning department and ask to look at objections as soon as the objection period has passed. Speak to an officer if you are not clear about any objections.

If an adverse objection has been made, get a written representation submitted quickly. It is unlikely that an inspector or district council will refuse to take into account your views in such circumstances. Both have discretion to entertain late comments and the council will usually welcome support for the Plan in the face of an objection that it will be fighting.

Once you establish someone has made an objection that you want to oppose, you could speak to the person or organization who made it, but, as with planning applications, if you are fundamentally against what objectors put forward there is probably little point in contacting them.

Whilst there is little for objectors to lose by pursuing an objection vigorously, they usually prefer not to be opposed by members of the public and so can be prepared to talk. If objectors are willing to discuss their case, you might be able to agree concessions. In this event, ensure their objection is formally modified. This can be done by the objector writing to the district council or at the Local Plan inquiry.

MAKING YOUR OBJECTIONS

Of the two main stages for making comments to the council on a Local Plan, the consultation draft is where the council is looking for feedback on its ideas. Public pressure is more likely to be effective here than later, because the council's proposed policies will not be so firmly entrenched. Weight of numbers has a far greater effect on councillors than on a Local Plan inspector.

On the other hand, the deposit draft is the more formal part of the procedure. This is your opportunity to challenge the council's views, with the Local Plan inspector to judge the planning merits of the case.

Consultation drafts

When the Local Plan is first published it will contain information on when and where to make comments. There might be a simple form that you can use or, if you prefer, write a letter. If you want to put forward a comprehensive case now, there is nothing to stop you. Otherwise, all you need do is write to the council. In this letter you should:

- give the name of the Plan;
- identify the parts or policies you object to;
- say briefly why you object; and
- set out what additions or changes you want to see.

FIGURE 5.3 PROCEDURE FOR OBJECTING TO A LOCAL PLAN ON DEPOSIT

Submit objection	complete form, send to council during 6 week deposit period
Acknowledgement	council writes confirming receipt of your objection
Report to committee	planning officers write a report on your objection to the council's committee and council decides whether to modify Plan
Modifications	you are told if the council proposes modifications relevant to your objection
Questionnaire	council sends form asking how you want to support your objection
Preinquiry meeting	council appoints Programme Officer to administer inquiry Planning Inspectorate appoints inspector to hold inquiry meeting held for inspector to discuss inquiry arrangements with council and objectors
Objection statements	you send a statement of your case to the council council sends you their statement on your objection copies of both statements sent to the inspector
Inquiry programme	you are sent a timetable showing when you are due to present your objection at the inquiry
Inquiry	inspector hears your objection and council's case
Inspector's report and council's proposed modifications	council sends you the relevant extract from inspector's report and recommendation, and a statement on whether Plan is to be modified
Objections to modifications	complete form, send to council during 6 week objection period, objections resolved with or without another inquiry

This letter will be read by planning officers and reported to councillors with all other comments. Remember, encourage as many people as you can to write at this stage. It does not necessarily take an enormous number of letters to influence the council: for example, a site was allocated for commercial development in the consultation draft Wrexham Maelor Local Plan. Around twenty-five letters

FIGURE 5.4 A TYPICAL LOCAL PLAN OBJECTION FORM

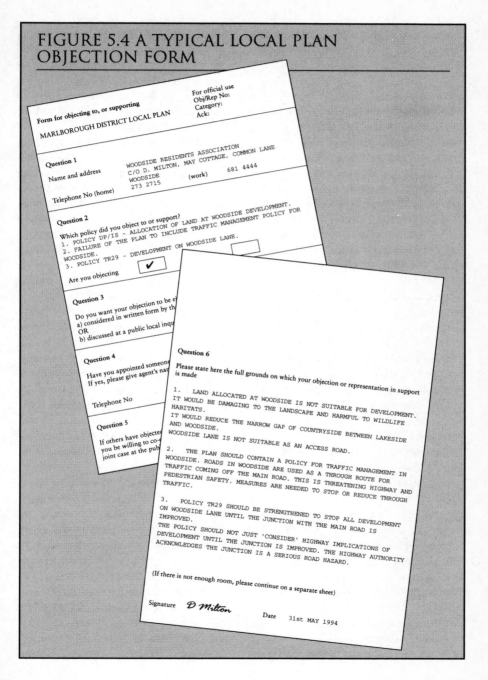

Form for objecting to, or supporting

MARLBOROUGH DISTRICT LOCAL PLAN

For official use
Obj/Rep No:
Category:
Ack:

Question 1

Name and address

WOODSIDE RESIDENTS ASSOCIATION
C/O D. MILTON, MAY COTTAGE, COMMON LANE
WOODSIDE

Telephone No (home)   273 2715   (work)   681 4444

Question 2

Which policy did you object to or support?
1. POLICY DP/IS - ALLOCATION OF LAND AT WOODSIDE DEVELOPMENT.
2. FAILURE OF THE PLAN TO INCLUDE TRAFFIC MANAGEMENT POLICY FOR WOODSIDE.
3. POLICY TR29 - DEVELOPMENT ON WOODSIDE LANE.

Are you objecting   ✔

Question 3

Do you want your objection to be e
a) considered in written form by th
OR
b) discussed at a public local inqu

Question 4

Have you appointed someone
If yes, please give agent's na

Telephone No

Question 5

If others have objecte
you be willing to co-
joint case at the pub

Question 6

Please state here the full grounds on which your objection or representation in support is made

1.   LAND ALLOCATED AT WOODSIDE IS NOT SUITABLE FOR DEVELOPMENT. IT WOULD BE DAMAGING TO THE LANDSCAPE AND HARMFUL TO WILDLIFE HABITATS.
IT WOULD REDUCE THE NARROW GAP OF COUNTRYSIDE BETWEEN LAKESIDE AND WOODSIDE.
WOODSIDE LANE IS NOT SUITABLE AS AN ACCESS ROAD.

2.   THE PLAN SHOULD CONTAIN A POLICY FOR TRAFFIC MANAGEMENT IN WOODSIDE. ROADS IN WOODSIDE ARE USED AS A THROUGH ROUTE FOR TRAFFIC COMING OFF THE MAIN ROAD. THIS IS THREATENING HIGHWAY AND PEDESTRIAN SAFETY. MEASURES ARE NEEDED TO STOP OR REDUCE THROUGH TRAFFIC.

3.   POLICY TR29 SHOULD BE STRENGTHENED TO STOP ALL DEVELOPMENT ON WOODSIDE LANE UNTIL THE JUNCTION WITH THE MAIN ROAD IS IMPROVED.
THE POLICY SHOULD NOT JUST 'CONSIDER' HIGHWAY IMPLICATIONS OF DEVELOPMENT UNTIL THE JUNCTION IS IMPROVED. THE HIGHWAY AUTHORITY ACKNOWLEDGES THE JUNCTION IS A SERIOUS ROAD HAZARD.

(If there is not enough room, please continue on a separate sheet)

Signature   *D Milton*   Date   31st MAY 1994

opposing the allocation persuaded the borough council to take it out when the Plan was revised.

Deposit drafts

Formal objections (against some aspect of the Plan) or representations (supporting some aspect of the Plan) must be made while the Local Plan is on deposit (see Figure 5.3). If you want to seek professional advice on a Local Plan, this is the time to do so (see Appendix I). Your consultant should fill in any forms on your behalf.

If you prefer to make your own objections or representations, fill in the Local Plan objection form provided by the district council (see Figure 5.4). If you object to more than one aspect of the Plan, you are usually asked to use a separate sheet for each objection.

There are no dire consequences if you complete this official-looking form; objecting to a Local Plan is not a legalistic business. The process is there to allow members of the public to get involved, and you are not committing yourself to anything further.

On the form fill in the policy reference and related paragraph numbers of the policy you object to or support (you should have a note of these from when you studied the Plan). Remember, you can object on the basis that the Plan should include additional policies. In this event, say you object to the failure of the Plan to include a policy on whatever subject it is. Put which section of the Plan it should go into.

Then decide whether a written case will suffice or whether you would prefer to take part in the Local Plan inquiry. Look back to pages 70–4 to get an idea of what an inquiry is like. Where your arguments are complex or need explanation and discussion, opt for the inquiry. If you are not sure, opt for the inquiry anyway. You can revert back to just a written statement later, if you change your mind.

Whatever you say on the form about appointing someone to act as your agent does not stop you deciding to get help later on. If you have agreed to represent other objectors, they should put your name here. There is usually a question about working together with people who object to the same policies as you. Unless you have a particular reason for not doing so, answer 'yes'. This does not commit you to anything or restrict what you can do.

The most important part of the form is the section dealing with your reasons for objecting or supporting. This is the equivalent of grounds of appeal for a planning appeal or a short letter of objection to a planning application. The reasons you give can be brief but must be clearly stated and on the relevant planning points so they let the council know what concerns you and what changes you want to see in the Plan. You can expand on these reasons later. If you make a representation in support of a plan, to oppose someone else's objection, and you want to speak at the inquiry, say so now. Add a note at the bottom of the form. Keep a copy of the completed Local Plan objection form for your records. Be sure to send the original to the district council within the objection period – the full address is usually on the form or in the attached notes.

Each separate objection is given a reference number by the council, which you will be told. A copy of your objection form will be available for public inspection with all the other objections made.

If you do not want to do any more, just filling in the objection form can be the end of your active participation in the Local Plan. It is not so daunting that your supporters should be put off registering their opposition too.

Local Plans attract varying numbers of objections: only one hundred objections were made to Wansbeck District Local Plan, which is an unusually low number, while East Lindsay Local Plan in Lincolnshire attracted two thousand comments. Unless every objector is happy to put his case in writing, there will be a Local Plan inquiry. It is very unusual for there not to be one. The district council appoints a programme officer, who is a council employee. His function is to administer objections and to liaise between the Local Plan inspector, district council and objectors.

Some time after you send in your Local Plan objection form, the planning officer will contact you. If he thinks there is scope to negotiate over your objections a meeting will be arranged. If you reach agreement, the officer should put forward a modification. The inspector considers this together with all other suggested changes to the Plan. Where you do not reach agreement, or only partially, press on with your objection. You can explain how far you have reached agreement in your objection statement or at the inquiry.

In any event, the council sends you another form to find out how you are going to back up your objection and whether you withdraw some or all of your objections. You have to say whether you want to rely

on your objection form, add to the objection in writing or speak at the inquiry. If you intend taking part in the inquiry, record on the form whether you intend to deal with the objection personally, use a consultant or advocate, and whether you are going to have other expert witnesses (planning consultant, highway engineer, landscape architect or others). Return the completed form to the council by the date specified, taking a copy for your records. Unless you intend to rely on your objection form alone, you now need to think about preparing your case.

Objection statements

Whether you plan to attend the Local Plan inquiry or explain your reasons in writing, you need to draw up an objection statement – but not necessarily immediately. You should be told by the programme officer or at a preinquiry meeting (see below) when statements should be submitted. A date is also set for the district council to produce its statement in response to your objection.

If you want to comment on another objector's case but have not had the opportunity to do so by the due date, still send your statement to the council on time. Look at the objector's case afterwards and make comments on it in writing or at the inquiry. If you want to speak at the inquiry, however, you do not have to submit a statement, but people supporting the Plan do not have an automatic right to take part. It is better to say something in writing than to miss the opportunity altogether.

Representations in favour of the Plan and against other objections can be slightly more difficult than objections to the

Plan itself. Before you embark on writing a long and detailed statement, speak to the planning officers. Find out what they intend doing. There is no point in duplicating effort yet the district council cannot be relied on to fight every objection. It might, on reflection, agree with some and argue for a modification to its own draft Plan in line with the objection. It is the Plan as published that is the starting point for the Local Plan inspector's consideration so make sure you know the council's reaction.

A Local Plan objection statement is similar to a letter of objection to a planning application or to written representations on a planning appeal, except that with applications and appeals you are reacting to aspects of a specific proposal (see pages 40–7 and 66–9). Local Plans deal with development at a more general level. Land allocated for development might be no more than a line drawn around the site on a proposals map. Policies set guidance for the sort of situations in which certain types of development would be allowed. You must think about the implications of policies at this general level. Points such as overlooking neighbouring properties, design and site layout are seldom relevant to Local Plans.

There is no set length or form for a Local Plan objection statement. It could be a letter on two or three sides of A4 paper. Concise, clear statements are the most effective, including any plans, drawings, photographs and illustrations that might be helpful to your case.

Start your statement with an introduction setting out what your objection relates to and mentioning if you represent a group or other individual objectors. Where you object to the Plan because it does not include policies that you feel it should, try to come up with a succinct statement of the policy that you want to see put into the Local Plan. Then go on to location and description. Where your objection is about a particular site, describe where it is, what it is like and the surrounding area. Where you object to a policy that applies to a wide area or throughout the district, describe the relevant characteristics: for example, where a policy affects development in an existing residential area, describe its character and the features that you want to see preserved.

The history and development of the town or district could be helpful to your case; if it has a bearing on the issues, put it in. In the background section of a statement you can also deal with existing and past uses of a site and any previous planning decisions. Remember, planning applications and appeals might have been turned down on points of detail rather than underlying principle.

Include a section in your objection statement on planning policy if it is relevant as Local Plan policies should be consistent with each other, the county Structure Plan and general government planning policy. Although the county council itself looks at the Local Plan to check it generally conforms to the Structure Plan, there might still be points to draw from Structure Plan policies.

In the issues and conclusions section draw all the information together to form a compelling case for what you propose. Say what changes should be made to improve the Plan or what defects need correcting.

When your statement is finished, ask the programme officer how many copies to send. The council will pass one copy to the inspector and make one copy available for the public. Keep at least one copy for yourself.

If you are not taking part in the Local Plan inquiry, that is all you need do until the Local Plan inspector's report is published months later. The council will contact you to let you know the result of your objection. There are steps you can take then (see pages 106–7).

LOCAL PLAN INQUIRIES

Although objections and representations are made to the district council, it is the Local Plan inspector who considers these, either at a Local Plan inquiry or in writing. His or her recommendations are very important, yet not binding on the district council.

A Local Plan inquiry is very similar to a planning appeal inquiry (see pages 70–4). The main difference is that at a Local Plan inquiry numerous objections are discussed and consequently it can last many weeks or even months. It also tends to be less formal: objectors often take part without being represented by professionals. The system is supposed to allow full public participation, and inspectors and planning officers do their best to make it as easy for you as they can.

If you do not want to speak at the Local Plan inquiry, that is fine – your written statement is taken into account by the inspector – or you can turn up at the inquiry as an observer. Taking part, however, does give you the opportunity to put questions to the council and to other objectors.

Regardless of whether you are familiar with inquiries, it is worthwhile attending the preinquiry meeting. If you have made an objection, you will be notified of this in advance. You can pick up useful pointers to the character of the inspector and how he wants to deal with things. Comply with this as far as possible. The inspector will also say when statements should be submitted prior to an objection being discussed at the inquiry. It is not, however, appropriate to go into the merits of individual cases at the preinquiry meeting.

Do not worry if you cannot make it to this meeting. The programme officer usually writes up notes and you can get a copy. He then sends a timetable for the Local Plan inquiry to all objectors. This shows when each objector is due to appear at the inquiry and how much time is allotted to discuss the objection. Contact the programme officer immediately if you cannot attend at the time allocated to you.

Where you make more than one objection, it is possible that you have to turn up at the inquiry more than once. Inquiry timetables are often arranged around main issues so that all discussion on a particular topic takes place only once.

If you definitely want to speak out against someone else's objection at the Local Plan inquiry, raise this at the preinquiry meeting or let the programme officer know in advance. You also need to check when the objection in question is going to be discussed.

Presenting your objections

By the time you appear at the Local Plan

inquiry you should have submitted your arguments in writing. If the district council opposes your objection, you should have received its statement. Study this thoroughly, in the way recommended on pages 60–4. If there are points in the council's statement you do not understand, speak to the planning officer about them before you attend the inquiry. There might be points that you need to check or further work to do. Remember to make notes ready for your questions.

At the Local Plan inquiry itself, the inspector will guide you through the process. If your own statement is short, you might be asked to read it out. Otherwise, you will be asked to summarize your case. This is to set the scene, especially for any members of the public who are present; the inspector and the planning officer will have read your statement already. When you finish your introduction you will be asked questions by the district council's advocate, usually a solicitor or barrister, and by the inspector. These can be about anything in your statement and points made by the council. The council's advocate will then present the district council's case, and you and the inspector can question the planning officer direct about it. The council's advocate sums up the council's case in support of the Plan as it is, or as the council has modified it. Fortunately, you have the last word. Briefly restate your best points and, if you can, mention anything helpful to your case that came out of the discussion at the inquiry. When you finish, the inspector will say that discussion about that objection is concluded. The inquiry then moves on to the next objection.

Opposing other objections

When you want to oppose someone else's objection at the Local Plan inquiry, you should have already made a representation in support of the Plan policy. You might also have sent a written statement to the council about the objection. This is given full weight by the inspector and council. Any support for the Plan is supposed to be dealt with in this way and the inspector is not bound to let you speak at the inquiry. Inspectors, however, have discretion on this. Normally, you have to show that you want to raise issues that the council is not going to. This means you need to contact the planning officers to find out what they will say and whether there is anything further you can add.

When the objection is dealt with at the inquiry, unless you have got agreement about speaking in advance, there is likely to be some discussion over whether you can take part. Be ready to distinguish what you want to say from what the council says.

The district council can agree with the objection, entirely or in part, or oppose it. Their statement, which you might not be sent automatically, should make their stance clear. Contact the planning officer beforehand if you are in any doubt.

Objectors might be represented by a barrister and professional witnesses. They present their case first, the council will ask questions and you put yours. The council will then present its case; thereafter questions can be put to them by objectors or their representatives. You then have your say: give your own particular reasons for supporting the Plan as it stands and explain the disadvantages of the objectors' alternative. After the objectors have questioned you, the council will sum up its case. The objectors have the last word and the inspector closes discussion on that objection.

FIGURE 5.5 A TYPICAL INSPECTOR'S REPORT ON AN OBJECTION FOLLOWING A LOCAL PLAN INQUIRY

Introduction

This objection concerns the Local Plan provision and policies concerning open space within a largely urban Borough.

Commentary

4.67 I support the council's proposed changes to the open space policies which now appear to meet the objections to a great extent. The effect of the wildlife strategy has been considered and I believe the changed policies and supporting text agree with the council's aim to provide the best possible environment for residents without imposing strict restraints on the development needed to keep the town alive. Loss of public open space should be matched by new provision of at least equal standard. I understand the desire to protect private playing fields but the best use for each site should be a matter for detailed consideration when an application for development is made.

Recommendations

R312 page 72, Policy ENV35: delete the policy and replace with:
"PLANNING PERMISSION FOR THE DEVELOPMENT OF EXISTING PUBLIC OPEN SPACE WILL BE REFUSED UNLESS IT IS TO PROVIDE PUBLIC OR COMMUNITY RECREATIONAL FACILITIES FOR DEMONSTRATED NEEDS OR UNLESS EQUALLY VALUABLE REPLACEMENT PROVISION IS MADE UNDER PROPOSALS IN THIS PLAN. THE IMPACT OF SUCH FACILITIES ON THE TOWNSCAPE, LANDSCAPE AND LOCAL COMMUNITY WILL BE CAREFULLY ASSESSED."

R313 page 73, Policy ENV36: delete the policy and replace with:
"OPPORTUNITIES FOR CREATING FURTHER AMENITY SPACE AND NATURAL HABITATS WILL BE TAKEN THROUGH ENVIRONMENTAL IMPROVEMENT SCHEMES AND LANDSCAPING SCHEMES REQUIRED FOR NEW DEVELOPMENTS."

INSPECTORS' SITE VISITS

Local Plan site inspections generally take place after all objections have been heard, so this can be weeks after you discussed your objection. Objectors who take part in the inquiry normally attend the site visit, which is arranged by the programme officer – but not during your formal appearance at the inquiry itself. He will contact you later to arrange a date and time. You may not discuss the merits of a case at a Local Plan site visit.

THE DECISION

When all objections have been heard at the inquiry and site inspections made, the Local Plan inspector considers each case and reports his recommendations to the council (see Figure 5.5).

Inspector's report

The report, which can take anything between a few months and a year to write, sets out the inspector's findings on all objections. For each objection, or group of objections, there is a summary of the objector's case and the council's response. The inspector says what conclusion he or she has reached and whether he or she agrees with the Plan as it is or whether he or she recommends changes.

Planning officers go through the report, and draw up draft modifications. These are put to a planning committee for approval. This is another opportunity to speak to councillors and lobby for the changes you want as the council does not have to follow the inspector's recommendations – although in most cases it will.

Where the council does not follow an inspector's suggested changes to the Plan, his recommendation can still be relevant. If a subsequent planning application is made, the inspector's conclusion could be influential in the decision, particularly at an appeal.

The council should tell you whether it intends to change the Plan in the light of your objection and the inspector's report. It might send you the relevant part of the inspector's report. If it does not, go to the planning department and ask to see it. The inspector's report and list of proposed modifications, together with reasons for them, is available for public inspection. Read what the inspector said, what his conclusions are and whether he recommends any changes. See how the council's proposed changes, or lack of them, compare.

CHALLENGING DECISIONS

During the six-week period for objecting to modifications proposed by the planning officers, you can object to a modification proposed by the council as well as to the council's failure to modify where the inspector's report recommends that it should. You cannot, however, object to the original Plan again. Make your objection on the form the planning department provides, following the guidelines about making objections and representations on pages 101–5.

Sometimes another inquiry is held into objections to modifications. This happens when objections raise issues that were not considered previously, where the council puts forward new policies or where modifications made to meet objections are subsequently withdrawn. In most cases further inquiries do not take place.

If the council goes against an inspector's recommendation in your favour, or you think the Plan does not follow government policy, you can write to the Secretary of State urging him to direct the council to modify the Local Plan in some way. In more extreme cases, the Secretary of State can call in the whole Local Plan in the same way that planning applications can be called in. He does this when:

● the Local Plan does not appear to conform with national or regional policies or with the county Structure Plan;
● where it raises important issues on a national or regional scale;
● where it is very controversial, possibly affecting other areas; or

● where there are outstanding objections from the Ministry of Agriculture, Food & Fisheries.

South Cambridgeshire District Council, for example, was directed to change a policy putting restrictions on employment in a business park as this was contrary to government policy.

After objections to modifications have been dealt with, with or without an inquiry, councillors vote to adopt the Local Plan. This formal procedural step marks completion of the preparation of a Local Plan.

If you are still unhappy, Local Plans, like planning appeal decisions, can be challenged in the courts on limited grounds. Procedural complaints can also be investigated (see pages 76–7).

LOCAL PLANS – ACTION CHECK LIST

1 Find out from the council when a Local Plan is being prepared.
2 Check the dates for making comments and objections.
3 Study the plan and make notes.
4 Discuss your concerns and queries with a planning officer and stay in touch to monitor progress.
5 Lobby councillors and consultees.
6 Alert other potential objectors and the media.
7 Write a letter to the council at the consultation stage.
8 Complete and send an objection form to the council during the deposit period.
9 Draw up an objection statement and send it to the council.
10 Prepare for and attend the Local Plan inquiry.
11 Read the planning inspector's report and the council's statement and proposed modifications. Contact planning officers and councillors again.
12 Check the final result of your objection with the council.

Chapter 6

ROAD BUILDING AND
COMPULSORY PURCHASE

One of the most controversial types of development is new road
building – motorways, trunk roads, bypasses and relief roads –
because there is increasing concern over vehicle pollution and the
effects of roads themselves ploughing through countryside and
built up areas. Other large-scale development such as urban
regeneration projects and town centre redevelopment also affects
large numbers of people especially as, in many cases, it involves
compulsory purchase. Yet compensation will never fully reflect
the noise, dirt and disruption they suffer.

In this chapter we look at how to stop or influence road building and compulsory purchase. Other kinds of project follow broadly similar planning procedures, for example some power stations, long-distance pipelines, light railways, rights of way and pedestrianization. Some of the detail is different but most of this chapter is also relevant to them.

Trunk roads, motorways and a few other categories of large-scale development do not go through the normal planning application and appeals process. Special orders are made, which are the equivalent of planning permission. Public inquiries into these orders provide you with an opportunity to influence the decision. Where compulsory purchase orders are involved, this represents an additional opportunity, equally as important as planning applications and appeals. If the relevant order is not confirmed, the development cannot take place. In practice, it is often easier to challenge details of schemes rather than the principle so, before taking a proposal head-on, think whether some amendment could make it acceptable to you.

FINDING OUT ABOUT SPECIAL ORDERS

If your property is directly affected by road or compulsory purchase proposals, you should be notified about them. Otherwise, like planning applications and Local Plans, publicity can be very easily missed and it is therefore important that you keep your eyes open.

Notices about special orders such as road and compulsory purchase orders are published in local papers, which will run stories on larger schemes. Look out for leaflets and exhibitions about new roads, especially in planning departments and libraries.

The Department of Transport, the Scottish and Welsh Offices and Roads Service of the Northern Ireland DoE are responsible for trunk roads and motorways, which comprise the major road network. Two main types of road order are made: a line order, which establishes a route; and a side road order, which deals with alterations needed to existing roads as a result of the proposed new road. For administrative purposes, a proposed road is divided into sections, each with a number of different line and side road orders. Confirmation of a road order is the equivalent of planning permission. Even when confirmed, road orders do not give power to buy the land needed to carry out the scheme. County councils and district councils deal with roads other than trunk roads and motorways. These must have planning permission and are publicized like other types of planning application.

Road proposals are included in county Structure Plans and Local Plans, which can be read at the council's planning department. Look at the key diagram and proposals map where the routes are shown. The sections of plans dealing with highways and transport set out any new road building or improvements. Ask at either the county council highways or planning departments or at the district council planning department for information about road building in the area.

The power to buy land is dealt with separately by compulsory purchase orders. In these, a variety of public authorities can

THE NONHAM-GODLEIGH TRUNK ROAD (GREENHILL TO OLDBURY SECTION) COMPULSORY PURCHASE ORDER (NO. ME 16)

SCHEDULE 1

Number on Plan	Extent, description and situation of the land	Owners or reputed owners	Lessees or reputed lessees	Occupiers (other than tenants for a month or less)
	In the Parish of Oldbury in the District of West Godleigh			
10/1	22,000 sq metres All of the property known as Stables House, Oldbury (OS XX 9170)	L Grant Stables House Stone Lane Oldbury		Owner
10/2	12,000 sq metres Pasture land and footpath 3a, east of Timberwood, Oldbury (Part OS XX 9268)	Mrs H Newman Layfield Farm Oldbury	P James New House Rabbit Hill Oldbury	Lessee
10/3	14,300 sq metres Arable land, east of Timberwood, Oldbury (Part OS XX 9280)	ditto		Owner
10/4	11,200 sq metres Rough grass land and woodland, east of Hill Rise, Oldbury (OS XX 9028)	W Briant 23 West Bank Nonham		J Martin 17 Timberwood Oldbury
10/5	250 sq metres Part of garden and outbuilding of Hazelwood, Rabbit Hill Lane, Oldbury (Part OS XX 8716)	Mr & Mrs Edmonds Hazelwood Rabbit Hill Lane Oldbury		Owner

When a compulsory purchase order is made, it is accompanied by a schedule on the lines of this one for the Nonham–Godleigh trunk road.

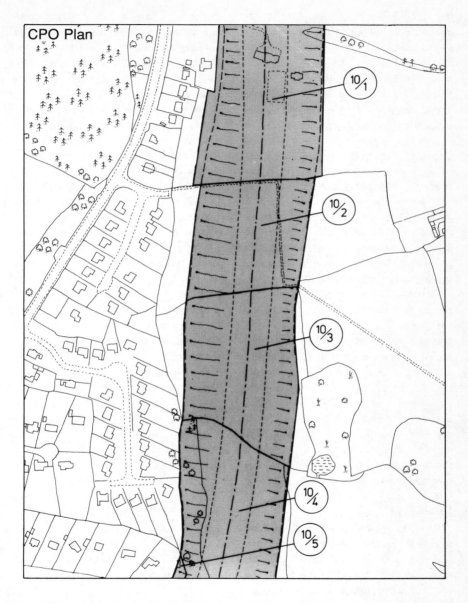

Plans attached to a compulsory purchase order show the land to be acquired for that development.

buy land or buildings regardless of the owner's wish to sell. When councils want to buy land they usually get planning permission before trying to make compulsory purchase orders. Whether or not you objected to the planning application, it should alert you to the possibility of a subsequent compulsory purchase order.

When you hear that draft road or compulsory purchase orders have been published, go and look at them. The official notice of the order should say where copies can be seen. If your land is involved, you should be sent a notice saying where the order can be seen. Contact the Department of Transport regional office or the council if you experience any problem in seeing the documents.

A special order is a legalistic document, which might mean very little to you. More important, for your objection, is the plan and statement of reasons for making the order, which are really no different to a location plan and statement in support of a planning application. The plan shows the land affected by the order; the statement describes the background and need for the underlying development. Ask for a photocopy of these and study them, assessing the proposal exactly as you would a planning application (see pages 25–35).

OBJECTIONS

With road and compulsory purchase proposals you should object as strongly as possible, as early as possible. The further a scheme gets, the harder it is to change, so, in the case of trunk roads, mount a vigorous campaign at the public participation stage (see Figure 6.1). This worked in the case of the A3 improvements at Hindhead, Surrey. Campaigners succeeded in getting the Department of Transport to agree to a tunnel under Hindhead Common, avoiding the attractive Devil's Punch Bowl and a Site of Special Scientific Interest.

Mobilize as many people as you can to voice their opposition, using the press, leaflets and local amenity groups (see pages 47–52). Speak to councillors – parish, district and county – as they, too, can be objectors to trunk roads. The London Borough of Waltham Forest campaigned as far as the High Court against a six-lane extension to the M11 between Hackney Wick and Leytonstone. With development other than trunk roads you could have many chances to object: such as when the Local Plan is being prepared or when a planning application is being submitted. Make sure that you do not miss those opportunities because you stand more chance of success at those stages because it is easier to influence your council than an inspector. A petition of 2,393 signatures objecting to a section of the Luton East Circular Road was submitted when the Luton Borough Local Plan was published as objectors were concerned about the effect on landscape, natural history and archaeology.

If you do not succeed at the Local Plan or planning application stage, keep the pressure up, particularly on councillors. Campaigning between formal planning decisions might persuade the council not to press on to subsequent stages.

Objection letters

When draft road or compulsory purchase orders are published, you have at least six

FIGURE 6.1 PROCEDURE FOR APPROVING A NEW TRUNK ROAD

Programme	Department of Transport (DTp) includes proposed new road in national Road Programme
Proposed routes	engineers identify possible routes; confidential consultation with official bodies
Public participation	alternative routes published for public comment
Preferred route	DTp announces its chosen alternative
Draft orders	DTp draws up and publishes road orders; environmental statement published, compulsory purchase order can be published at same time
Objections	owners of property affected and anyone else can write to relevant Secretary of State objecting to road order
Public inquiry arranged	DTp notifies objectors of date and venue 6 weeks before public inquiry and sends statement of reasons for orders 4 weeks before inquiry; notice of inquiry published in newspapers and site notices put up 2 weeks before inquiry
Public inquiry	independent inspector hears DTp and objectors cases and reports to relevant Secretary of State
Decision	Relevant Secretary of State considers report, confirms, modifies or rejects order; decision letter sent to objectors
Purchase	DTp draws up associated side road orders and compulsory purchase orders to implement scheme

weeks in which to object (see Figure 6.2). Your formal, written objection should give your grounds for objecting. A short letter is all that is needed, similar in content to one objecting to a Local Plan (see pages 101–3). Make clear precisely what it is you object to (see Figure 6.3). You might:

● be against the very principle and not want the development to go ahead in any form;

● accept the underlying need for, or desirability of, the development but feel it is not in the right place. With roads, you can argue for different routes. With other

FIGURE 6.2 PROCEDURE FOR APPROVING A COMPULSORY PURCHASE ORDER

Negotiation	council tries to buy property by agreement with owners
Resolution	council officers recommend compulsory purchase order (cpo) used; councillors vote to make draft cpo
Ownership research	council finds out who owns/occupies property; notice served on owners asking details of ownership
Draft orders	council draws up cpo, notifies owners and publishes notice in newspaper for 2 weeks
Objections	owners and anyone else can write to relevant Secretary of State objecting to cpo
Submission	council sends draft cpo to relevant Secretary of State
Notice of public inquiry	Secretary of State notifies council and objectors of public inquiry; within 6 weeks council sends case for cpo to objectors
Public inquiry	objectors informed of date and venue 6 weeks before public inquiry; council publishes notice in newspaper and puts up site notice 2 weeks before inquiry; independent inspector hears council and objectors cases and reports to relevant Secretary of State
Decision	Secretary of State considers report, confirms, modifies or rejects cpo; decision letter sent to council and objectors
Advert	council publishes notice of cpo in newspaper; cpo comes into effect after 6 weeks
Purchase	council begins to buy property; owners claim compensation

compulsory purchase orders, you can argue for an alternative site; or
● accept both the scheme and its chosen location, but object to some details.

If your property is directly affected you can object to its inclusion, suggest the project can take place without it or seek some amendment to protect your interests. Bear in mind, you are more likely to secure a change in a detail than to overturn the whole scheme.

The notice of the road or compulsory purchase order gives the address to which

FIGURE 6.3 AN EFFECTIVE LETTER OF OBJECTION TO A ROAD OR COMPULSORY PURCHASE ORDER

Secretary of State
Regional Office

ref: 23879/rd/7365443/TS   16 October 1993

Dear Sir

THE NONHAM–GODLEIGH TRUNK ROAD
(GREENHILL TO OLDBURY SECTION) ORDER

I wish to lodge a formal objection to this order.

My reasons for objecting are as follows:

1. There will be serious harmful effects on the adjoining residential area, in particular Timberwood, Hill Rise and Rabbit Hill Lane, by virtue of noise, fumes and visual impact.

2. Important trees and woodland which contribute to the character of the area will be lost.

3. The landscape of an Area of Outstanding Natural Beauty will be significantly harmed by cuttings, re-grading and the appearance of the road.

4. An important local building will be demolished.

5. Alternative routes are available which would minimize the harmful effects noted above.

As my property is included I am a statutory objector and understand that my objection means a public inquiry must be held into the order. I reserve the right to add to and elaborate on my reasons for objection at the public inquiry.

Yours faithfully

L Grant

---

your objection letter should be sent and also the date by which it should be received. Try to meet the deadline but write anyway if you are outside the specified time. Urge as many people as possible to send objections, but make it easy for them. Supply the address, deadline and indicate the sort of thing to say.

Whether you decide to rely on a written objection or go to the inquiry, you can draw up a written objection statement. We now look at the case against road proposals and then at compulsory purchase orders.

Objection statements on road proposals

From your knowledge of the proposed route of the new road you can work up your case on what we might describe as normal planning grounds: environmental effect, visual impact, loss of historic buildings, effect on wildlife habitats and road safety.

What you might not be able to find out until nearer the inquiry is the technical justification for proposing the road. These are the traffic figures and forecasts prepared for the Department of Transport or council. Eventually traffic models will be produced, which show the distribution and levels of vehicles using existing and proposed road networks.

Contact the regional office of the Department of Transport or council concerned to find out what information it can supply. Ask about traffic counts it has carried out and about different schemes proposed in the past, which have since been abandoned.

Traffic studies might have been published at the public participation stage, when exhibitions and meetings are held and questionnaires invite public views on a proposal. These studies could relate to each of the alternatives originally considered and one of these might be preferable to you. The Department of Transport or council should be able to supply copies. The information could be slightly out of date but at least it gives you something to work on.

Whatever technical material you can get hold of is likely to be completely incomprehensible, certainly at first so ask an officer of the Department of Transport or council to explain it. This is one area to think seriously about getting professional help.

You do not have to tackle the technical traffic aspects but can instead concentrate on planning grounds. Draw up your statement as you would for a planning appeal or Local Plan objection (see pages 66–9 and 101–3). Deal with all the factors that are relevant to the road proposal in question.

A landscape appraisal of the road is carried out for the Department of Transport or council, but this too might not be available until near the inquiry date. Get hold of it as soon as you can and go through it looking for ammunition to use against the scheme and for flaws in the assessment.

Your objection stands more chance of success if you can put forward an alternative road proposal. You do not have to go into great detail – just show the line of the road on a scale map – yet to be really effective the alternative must be realistic. If you can, put forward a scheme that complies with Department of Transport or highways authority standards for carriageway widths and layouts, junctions and slip roads, gradients, curves and alignment. Again, this is getting very technical so think about getting advice from a highway engineer.

Cooperate with other objectors clubbing together to get professional help and, if possible, by all arguing for the same alternative route or changes. This makes it easier for the inspector, and it also avoids other objectors criticizing your proposed route.

Individual road proposals arise from and are judged against government policy on national road and transport policy. You might have fundamental objections to government road policy on, for example, Department of Transport traffic growth figures; the amount of new road building and its cost; the merits of public transport; the general increase in cars on the road; and inefficient use of the world's resources. These wider issues, however, will not be taken into account by the inspector at an inquiry into a specific road proposal and so will not influence the decision. Your case must concentrate on the details of the particular road scheme and the effect on its setting.

Do not be put off objecting to a road proposal: it is a type of development like any other. The difference is that you have additional traffic grounds on which to oppose it.

Side road orders

On side road orders, your objections should be more constrained because the side roads must, of course, tie in with the new main road. Once the line of a road is confirmed, it cannot be challenged again when side road orders are made. The Society for the Preservation of the Battle of Naseby tried to stop the M1–A1 link when the related side road orders were considered. The route crossed the southern-most part of the battlefield, including the line of Prince Rupert's charge. The link road had, however, already been established and could not be objected to.

Objection statements on compulsory purchase orders

Your objection statement on a compulsory purchase order should be similar to one against a planning appeal or Local Plan (see pages 66–9 and 101–3). Ensure you know exactly what the council is proposing and how much detail it has gone into. If you do not know already, find out from the planning department whether the proposed development has been through the Local Plan process or has been given planning permission. Where it has, ask to see copies of all relevant documents:

- Local Plan;
- objections made to the Plan;
- inspector's report on objections to the Local Plan;
- planning application;
- officer's report to committee;
- objection letters; and
- decision notice.

Use all that information to help frame your objection statement by seeing what issues were raised, what arguments were used and how successful they were. This should give you useful pointers. Do not necessarily rule out lines of argument that have been rejected previously. The council makes the decisions on Local Plans and its own planning applications. An inspector could take a different view. Try to come up with as many new points as possible.

The council is supposed to set out the basis of its case in a statement and make it available at the council's offices six weeks after the Department of Environment confirms an inquiry is to be held or at least twenty-eight days before the inquiry

Despite cutting back its road programme in April 1994, in the face of public pressure, the government still plans to build thousands of miles of roads. Inevitably, further road building will be proposed in sensitive places such as this Area of Outstanding Natural Beauty.

starts. Get hold of the council's case as early as possible.

NEGOTIATING WITH THE AUTHORITIES

Once you submit your objection to a road or compulsory purchase order, and particularly if your property is directly affected, Department of Transport or council officers might contact you. As they want to minimize the number of objections they have to deal with, the officers might try to agree concessions with you. So much the better if this can be done – but beware. Do not withdraw your objections, or some of your objections, unless you get firm guarantees. This could be a statement to the inspector putting forward concessions that you have agreed, as an amendment to the scheme.

Do not rely on vague promises or letters written to you by the Department of Transport or council. If you are in any doubt, maintain your objection but write again setting out what you are prepared to agree to. Send this to the address you sent the original objection to.

PUBLIC INQUIRIES

About 450 public inquiries take place each year in England and Wales into various road orders, compulsory purchase orders and other similar types of orders. These inquiries are conducted by so-called 'independent' inspectors. Although administered by the Planning Inspectorate in England and Wales, these inspectors are theoretically nominated to hold inquiries by the Lord Chancellor so that they are seen to be independent of government departments. In practice, independent inspectors are like planning inspectors who hold planning appeal, Local Plan and other planning inquiries.

Public inquiries into objections to road and compulsory purchase are generally similar to all other inquiries (see pages 70–4 and 103–5). We concentrate in this section on the main differences.

If you make an objection you are told whether there is to be an inquiry, and when and where it is to be held. Inquiries can last for weeks, but you do not have to go along every day. Go on the first day, especially where there was no preinquiry meeting, to hear how the inquiry is to be dealt with and the timetable for objectors to speak. Where there are lots of objections or the inquiry will run for many weeks, a preinquiry meeting may be held. You should be sent notification of the preinquiry meeting and a list of what the inspector wants to discuss. Go to the meeting if you can.

Find out at the preinquiry meeting or on the first day of the inquiry itself when you will be able to question witnesses about the proposal. Decide which witnesses you want to question and when.

Only objectors whose property is included in the order have the legal right to take part at inquiries. In practice, however, all objectors are given the chance to participate, but as with other inquiries the inspector will not let you just repeat what others say so coordinate your action with others to avoid this.

Whether your property is actually included in the order can affect what documents you get sent. The Department of Transport or council should, for example, send you a statement of its case or tell you where you can see one. Full statements from the Department of Transport or council witnesses such as planning officers, highway engineers, surveyors or landscape architects should also be available a few weeks before the inquiry. Contact the Department of Transport regional office, or council, depending on who is making the order to find out the name and telephone number of the person who is making the arrangements. Check when and where you can see the witnesses statements and on any other inquiry arrangements on which you are unsure.

At the inquiry itself, the Department of Transport or council usually speaks first and also has the last word. Its opening introduction contains useful information but the full case could last for days so, for a large and complex inquiry try to arrange with other objectors to have someone present as much of the time as possible.

The presentation of your case and questions to witnesses should be the same as for other inquiries (see pages 72–4). If you put forward alternatives to what is being proposed, be ready to defend them. You will be asked questions designed to show your alternatives would not work or be as good as the proposed scheme.

THE DECISION

After the inquiry closes, the inspector writes a report to the appropriate Secretary of State summarizing the cases of the parties, reaching conclusions and making recommendations. The Secretary of State's department considers the report and writes a decision letter on behalf of the Secretary of State, like an appeal decision letter. The actual decision is to confirm the order, modify it or reject it.

If you objected, you should be sent a copy of the decision letter; read it carefully, noting the reasons for the decision. Even where an order is defeated, it is possible objections can be overcome by a different scheme.

Decisions on roads and compulsory purchase orders can be challenged in the courts. Complaints can also be made about the way the inquiry was handled or officers conducted themselves (see pages 76–7).

COMPENSATION

Costs incurred in attending or employing professional help at an inquiry can be claimed in limited circumstances: you must have land included in the draft compulsory purchase order and your objection must be successful or partly successful. If you think this applies to you, write to the government department whose address is on the decision letter or, if you qualify for legal aid, contact your local Citizens Advice Bureau or legal aid office.

Beyond those costs, you can claim compensation if any of your land is compulsorily purchased, so as soon as you find out your land is included in a compulsory purchase order, get advice from a chartered surveyor with experience in making compensation claims. Assessing compensation is carried out completely separately from the planning and order-making procedures. Neither the inquiry inspector nor the Secretary of State who makes the final decision can deal with your right to claim compensation or the level of payment. Compensation is based on the value of property that is taken away from you, the reduction in value of any property that you keep, and all the expenses you incur as a result of your property being compulsorily purchased. In virtually all cases, however, compensation is far less than the true value of what you lose; payments do not reflect the months of anguish and inconvenience that you suffer.

ROAD BUILDING AND COMPULSORY PURCHASE – ACTION CHECK LIST

1 Ask at the district council about any road or compulsory purchase proposals. Look out for publicity.
2 Get information about the scheme from the Department of Transport or council.
3 Campaign vigorously at the public participation stage of road orders.
4 Alert other potential objectors and the media.
5 Lobby councillors to oppose orders.
6 Find out the dates of the objection period and submit your objection letter.
7 Write a statement in support of your objection.
8 Prepare for and attend the inquiry.
9 Read the decision letter.

Chapter 7

SPECIAL DESIGNATIONS

Some areas and buildings are subject to special designations for planning purposes, and we now look more closely at some of the most common ones: Tree Preservation Orders, Green Belts, National Parks, Areas of Outstanding Natural Beauty, Sites of Special Scientific Interest, Conservation Areas, Listed Buildings, archaeological sites and those under 'article 4' directions. Such special cases not only attract additional planning restrictions in themselves but also receive more protection from neighbouring development proposals that might jeopardize their special qualities.

The special designations, or cases, described in this chapter have their basis in planning law. There are others that you might come across in a Local Plan and council's planning policy documents that do not have the same legal status as they are just informal designations created by the council itself (see pages 13–14).

TREE PRESERVATION ORDERS

Tree Preservation Orders (TPOs) are made to protect trees that have amenity value, that is they make a valuable contribution to the surrounding area. They can be put on single trees, small groups, areas or whole woodlands, yet planning law does not define a tree for TPO purposes. This can cause problems where, for example, a TPO applies to an area of woodland, individual trees are not specified. What sizes and species are covered is debatable. It is generally said that, for TPO purposes, the word 'tree' should have its ordinary meaning: a perennial plant with a woody trunk and branches. TPOs, therefore, do not include bushes and shrubs. The order shows the position of the trees on a map and states the species (see Figure 7.1). Single trees and trees within groups are specified individually. Trees in Conservation Areas automatically have similar protection to TPO trees (see pages 131–4).

With a few exceptions, a TPO tree should not be cut down, topped, lopped, uprooted or damaged without the consent of the district council, which makes TPOs and keeps records of them.

Applications to carry out work on TPO trees are like planning applications: appli-cants identify the trees, say what work they want to do and give reasons for the work. TPO applications, however, do not have to be advertised. You can object to TPO applications in the same way as you would a planning application (see pages 35–47). Remember, however, that trees are not permanent: they have a natural life span and need occasional work to keep them healthy and safe.

A council can refuse an application to carry out work to a TPO tree or grant consent with conditions, such as the requirement to replant. An applicant can then appeal to the Secretary of State for the Environment, Secretary of State for Scotland, the Secretary of State for Wales or the Secretary of State for Northern Ireland. Shrewsbury and Atcham Borough Council, for example, refused permission to fell a 5.5 metre (18 foot) high protected oak tree stump that had had all its branches removed under a previous permission. The owner argued it did not have any amenity value but the council said it would grow again. The owner's appeal was dismissed.

In theory, TPOs are made to protect important trees, but, in practice, councils use TPOs to help stop development or to gain greater control over it. Developers, for example, often prefer to deal with clear sites. Their first job, sometimes before making a planning application, is to send in bulldozers to remove every living thing from a site. Preemptive TPOs can stop this: before selling off six cemeteries, Edinburgh District Council made TPOs covering all of the 2,000 trees in five of them, the remaining cemetery being protected by a TPO already.

FIGURE 7.1 A TYPICAL TREE PRESERVATION ORDER

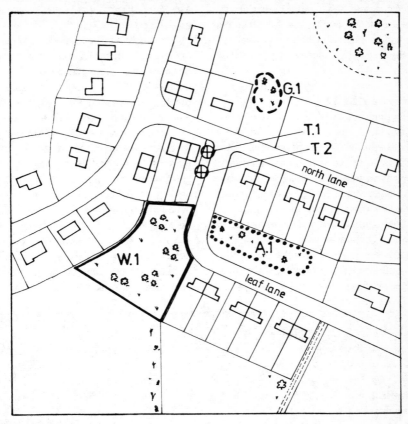

SCHEDULE	No. on map	Description	Situation

Trees specified individually (encircled in black on the map)

T.1	1 Oak		Land adj Leaf Lane, Branchley
T.2	1 Ash		As above

Trees specified by reference to an area (within dotted black line on the map)

A.1   Area consisting of scattered
specimens of Ash, Common Alder   As above

Groups of trees (within a broken black line on the map)

G.1   6 Ash   Land adj North Lane, Branchley

Woodlands (within a continuous black line on the map)

W.1   Mixed deciduous woodland
comprising: Oak, Ash,
Hornbeam, Cherry   As above

If work on TPO trees or other valuable trees is taking place and concerns you, telephone the landscape officer in the planning department to see whether permission is needed or has been given. He or she might be able to take immediate action.

GREEN BELTS

Green Belts are formally designated areas of land drawn around certain cities; the term 'Green Belt' does not mean any open countryside or the land surrounding every town, as is frequently believed. Only land that is to be kept permanently open should be included in a Green Belt.

The purposes of Green Belts are to stop urban sprawl, safeguard surrounding countryside, prevent towns merging, preserve the special character of historic towns and help urban regeneration. About 14 per cent of England is included in Green Belts; that around London alone covers well over 40,500 hectares (one million acres) (see Figure 7.2).

Green Belts are defined in development plans – their broad location in county Structure Plans and the detail of precise boundaries (usually features such as roads, streams and tree belts) in Local Plans. Therefore, if you want to have a say in what land is or is not included in a Green Belt, get involved in the preparation of the relevant Local Plan (see pages 89–97). Land allocated as part of the Green Belt is unlikely to be built on and, once established, the boundaries are not supposed to be changed.

Green Belts are controlled by strict planning policies that prevent all but a few limited types of development. They are the only place in which there is a general

---

FIGURE 7.2 GREEN BELTS IN THE UNITED KINGDOM

England		Scotland
Avon	Oxford	Aberdeen
Burton-Swadlincote	South West Hampshire/	Ayr/Prestwick
Cambridge	South East Dorset	Edinburgh
Gloucester, Cheltenham	South and West Yorkshire	Falkirk/Grangemouth
Greater Manchester,	Stoke-on-Trent	Greater Glasgow
Central Lancashire	Tyne & Wear	
Lancaster and Flyde	West Midlands	**Wales**
Coast	York	None
London		
Merseyside, Wirral		**Northern Ireland**
Nottingham, Derby		Belfast

presumption against development taking place. Except in very special circumstances, planning permission should not be given other than for agriculture and forestry, outdoor sports, cemeteries and institutions in extensive grounds. Mining and quarrying can be allowed where suitable environmental protection and restoration of the land is ensured. This does not, however, stop councils trying to release Green Belt land for development. For example, in drawing up its Unitary Development Plan, the City of Leeds proposed allocating a site in the Green Belt for a business park and 1,000 houses.

Where you are concerned with individual development proposals, inappropriate development in the Green Belt is a very powerful argument to use. Think how the proposal would affect the purposes of the Green Belt, and look in the Local Plan to see what the specific Green Belt policies are.

NATIONAL PARKS

National Parks are specially protected areas of attractive countryside in which the public are encouraged to seek enjoyment. Some 10 per cent of England and Wales is designated National Park, and the Norfolk and Suffolk broads, although not actually so designated, have the same status (see Figure 7.3). There are no National Parks as yet in Scotland or Northern Ireland.

National Parks are designated by the Countryside Commission and Countryside Council in Wales, with the approval of the government. They have their own authorities, which deal with planning matters and are like district councils. They draw up Local Plans covering the whole of

the National Park and decide planning applications in their area.

Inside National Parks, the types of development for which planning permission is automatically granted are more restricted (see page 11). There are thus no 'permitted development' rights for roof extensions, cladding the outside of houses, satellite dishes on chimneys, tall buildings and facing roads and for excavations for fish farming. There are also lower size limits for extensions to houses and industrial buildings and for building in the grounds of houses. Siting and design of extensions and alterations to agricultural buildings under the 'permitted development' regime can also be controlled by National Park authorities.

Look out for Local Plans being prepared for National Parks as National Park authorities are supposed to be working towards the 1996 deadline like district councils (see Chapter 5). See what is proposed and make your views on development in the Park known during that process. Local Plans for National Parks concentrate largely on conserving natural beauty but must also take into account the prosperity and social wellbeing of the area. The same factors come into play when planning applications are submitted. Apart from looking at the effect on scenery, proposals are expected to reflect traditional local styles of building and materials. The conversion of a stone building to a gamekeeper's cottage, for example, was not allowed in Brecon Beacons National Park. The site was in attractive open countryside close to a public footpath and conversion would not retain the character of the building. The gamekeeper's duties

FIGURE 7.3 NATIONAL PARKS, AREAS OF OUTSTANDING NATURAL BEAUTY AND NATIONAL SCENIC AREAS IN THE UNITED KINGDOM

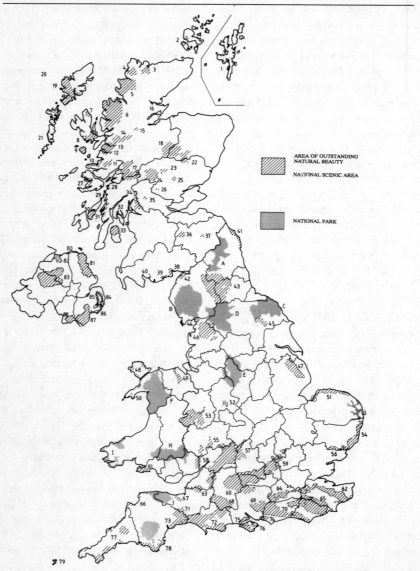

AREA OF OUTSTANDING
NATURAL BEAUTY

NATIONAL SCENIC AREA

NATIONAL PARK

FIGURE 7.3 (CONT.)

NATIONAL PARKS (ENGLAND AND WALES)

A	Northumberland	G	The Broads
B	Lake District	H	Brecon Beacons
C	North York Moors	I	Pembrokeshire Coast
D	Yorkshire Dales	J	Exmoor
E	Peak District	K	Dartmoor
F	Snowdonia		

NATIONAL SCENIC AREAS (SCOTLAND)

1	Shetland		
2	Hoy and West Mainland	21	South Uist Machair
3	Kyle of Tongue	22	Deeside and Lochnagar
4	N. W. Sutherland	23	Loch Tummel
5	Assynt-Coigach	24	Loch Rannoch and Glen Lyon
6	Wester Ross	25	River Tay (Dunkeld)
7	Trotternish	26	River Earn (Comrie to St Fillans)
8	The Cullin Hills	27	Loch na Keal, Isle of Mull
9	The Small Isles	28	Lynn of Lorn
10	Morar, Moidart and Ardnamurchan	29	Scarba, Lunga and the Garvellachs
11	Loch Shiel	30	Jura
12	Knoydart	31	Knapdale
13	Kintail	32	Kyles of Bute
14	Glen Affric	33	North Arran
15	Glen Strathfarrar	34	Loch Lomond
16	Dornoch Firth	35	The Trossachs
17	Ben Nevis and Glen Coe	36	Upper Tweedale
18	The Cairngorm Mountains	37	Eildon and Leaderfoot
19	South Lewis, Harris and North Uist	38	Nith Estuary
20	St Kilda	39	East Stewarty Coast
		40	Fleet Valley

FIGURE 7.3 (CONT.)

AREAS OF OUTSTANDING NATURAL BEAUTY

England & Wales

41	Northumberland Coast
42	Solway Coast
43	North Pennines
44	Arnside and Silverdale
45	Howardian Hills
46	Forest of Bowland
47	Lincolnshire Wolds
48	Anglesey
49	Clwydian Range
50	Llyen
51	Norfolk Coast
52	Cannock Chase
53	Shropshire Hills
54	Suffolk Coasts and Heaths
55	Malvern Hills
56	Dedham Vale
57	Cotswolds
58	Wye Valley
59	Chilterns
60	North Wessex Downs
61	Gower
62	Kent Downs
63	Mendip Hills
64	Surrey Hills
65	High Weald

66	North Devon
67	Quantock Hills
68	Cranborne Chase and West Wiltshire Downs
69	East Hampshire
70	Sussex Downs
71	Blackdown Hills
72	Dorset
73	East Devon
74	Chichester Harbour
75	South Hampshire Coast
76	Isle of Wight
77	Cornwall
78	South Devon
79	Isles of Scilly

Northern Ireland

80	Causeway Coast
81	Antrim Coast and Glen
82	North Derry
83	Sperrin
84	Strangford Lough
85	Langan Valley
86	Lecale Coast
87	Mourne
88	Ring of Gullion

were geared to sporting shoots, not strictly agriculture, and were only seasonal.

Large-scale development including mining and quarrying should only take place in National Parks in exceptional circumstances, and applicants must prove such development is in the public interest.

Three criteria apply:

- the need for the development nationally and locally;

- the opportunities for locating it somewhere outside the National Park or meeting the needs in a different way; and

- the degree of harm to the environment and landscape, and how that could be minimized.

So, for example, British Nuclear Fuels was given planning permission to drill test bore holes in the Lake District National Park as the survey information needed in connection with nearby Sellafield could not be collected in any other way.

Because National Parks are designated in recognition of the national importance of their landscape, you should develop your arguments for any objections along those lines. Assess the impact the proposal would have on the scenery and see how the proposed development would fit in with the existing buildings. The Countryside Commission and Countryside Council for Wales produce advice for development in National Parks so contact them to find out whether they have published anything relevant to your case (see page 146).

AREAS OF OUTSTANDING NATURAL BEAUTY

Like National Parks, Areas of Outstanding Natural Beauty (AONBs) are specially protected areas of countryside of national importance. The equivalent designation in Scotland is the National Scenic Area. In AONBs the needs of agriculture and other rural businesses and those of local communities still have to be taken into account, even though the primary purpose is to conserve and enhance natural beauty. Unlike National Parks, public access is not a criteria for an AONB; recreation is encouraged but only if it is compatible with conservation of natural beauty.

AONBs cover about 13 per cent of England and Wales (see Figure 7.3), and three further designations – Nidderdale, Tamar and Tavy valleys and Berwyn mountains –

are being considered.

County Structure Plans indicate the general location of an AONB and proposals maps in Local Plans show the boundaries. District councils also have even more detailed maps where you can check boundaries more precisely than in the Local Plan. AONB boundaries are not set through the Local Plan process. You cannot, therefore, get land near the edge of existing AONBs included through involvement in the Local Plan, nor can the district council itself designate new areas. You can, however, try to influence the Local Plan policies that apply in AONBs.

There are no special planning authorities for AONBs. Structure and Local Plans and the control of development are carried out by the county and district councils for the area, so that AONBs are covered by different planning authorities with slightly different planning policies. In addition to Structure and Local Plans, county and district councils often draw up informal policy documents for AONBs. These describe the features and character that make the area special and that need to be protected and set out the pressures on the area and what the councils plan to do to enhance the AONB.

The limits on 'permitted development' rights in National Parks also apply in AONBs (see page 125). Development allowed in AONBs is generally small scale, associated with the existing villages and properties or related to agriculture. The design and materials of new buildings are supposed to reflect local architecture and be situated unobtrusively, yet, in a controversial decision, the Secretary of State permitted a Centre Parcs holiday village in the AONB at Longleat, Wiltshire. The Council for the Protection of Rural England and Lovers of Longleat Association opposed it at the public inquiry but planning permission was granted because the development was an employment-generating tourism proposal, which was in the national interest. It would be contained within existing woods and involve further large-scale tree planting.

If a planning application that concerns you falls within an AONB, the designation will probably be an important factor in the decision. Find out what features of the landscape are recognized in planning policies and use your own judgment. Assess particularly the effect on these features and the impact on the views.

SITES OF SPECIAL SCIENTIFIC INTEREST

Sites of Special Scientific Interest (SSSIs) are areas designated to protect their wildlife or geological features. There are over 5,500 SSSIs in the United Kingdom covering roughly 8 per cent of the country. About 70 per cent of these are designated because of their wildlife value, about 19 per cent because of their geology, and the remainder for both reasons. In addition to SSSI status, some areas have extra designations (see Figure 7.4).

It is a criminal offence to carry out some activities in SSSIs without consent so owners and occupiers of SSSIs must notify English Nature, or the equivalent Scottish, Welsh and Northern Irish bodies, if they want to carry out the activities prohibited in the original SSSI notification. If you fear something is being done in or

near an SSSI which is causing damage, get in touch with the district council immediately. The officers can investigate and tell you whether the activity is allowed or take action to stop it. In an emergency, say at the weekend, you could contact the police.

Some 'permitted development' rights such as holding war games, motor sports and clay pigeon shoots are automatically restricted in SSSIs. District councils can also make formal directions that take away other 'permitted development' rights that might harm an SSSI.

If you think development proposals might affect an SSSI, check the Local Plan or ask about the site at the planning department. You can also ask to see the notification, which shows the location and extent of the designated site, and what its special features are. Note the features and the relevant planning policies and use these in your objections. Development is not banned completely but it is unusual for planning permission to be granted actually in SSSIs. It is more often the effect on nearby SSSIs that is the issue.

When a planning application is made for any development in an SSSI or for development outside but which might still affect it, English Nature, the Countryside Council for Wales, Scottish Natural Heritage or the Environment Service of the Northern Ireland DoE is consulted. Consultation areas are defined around SSSIs for this purpose. If a council decides to grant planning permission, against the advice of one of these conservation bodies, the latter can ask the Secretary of State to call in the application (see page 52).

FIGURE 7.4 ADDITIONAL NATURE CONSERVATION DESIGNATIONS THAT APPLY TO SOME SITES OF SPECIAL SCIENTIFIC INTEREST

National Nature Reserve	area of national or international importance controlled by English Nature, Scottish Natural Heritage or Nature Conservancy Council for Wales and used primarily for nature conservation
Special Protection Area	habitat of threatened bird species, part of European-wide 'Natura 2000' network of sites
Special Area of Conservation	habitat of endangered species, part of European-wide 'Natura 2000' network of sites
Ramsar Site	internationally important wetlands and habitat of waterfowl
Biogenetic Reserve	area for conservation of heathland and dry grassland
Marine Nature Reserve	area covered by tidal waters or sea for conservation of marine wildlife and geology

If a site or land that has some wildlife or geological interest is under threat of development, try to have it protected. Contact the local Wildlife Trust; the district council or your local library should have the address, if it is not in the telephone book. Alternatively, contact the officer who deals with nature conservation at the district council. He or she might be able to assist because district councils can establish Local Nature Reserves and make byelaws. Local Nature Reserves are not SSSIs but locally important wildlife habitats and their purpose is to conserve nature and provide the opportunity for the public to see wildlife. You could also contact English Nature or equivalent body (see page 146).

They will probably refer you to one of their regional offices.

CONSERVATION AREAS

Conservation Areas are parts of town and villages designated for their architectural or historic value (see Figure 7.5). By the early 1990s, there were more than 7,000 Conservation Areas, and new ones are being designated at a rate of 300–400 a year. Most large towns have at least one Conservation Area and all districts will have some: Cotswold District, Gloucester, has more than 130.

Conservation Areas vary widely in size. Some cover whole town centres, others just squares or small groups of buildings.

131

The features that justify the designation are also varied – buildings dating from the same period or of a uniform style, medieval street patterns, areas around village greens and parks – but each area must possess its own special character. Listed Buildings often form the core of Conservation Areas (see pages 134–6).

Such areas have tighter planning controls than areas not so designated. Permission, called Conservation Area consent, is needed to demolish part or all of most buildings and structures. An application, like a planning application, is made to the council, usually at the same time as planning permission is applied for. Planning applications for development that would affect the character or appearance of a Conservation Area must be advertised in a local newspaper and site notices put up. Any proposed felling or other work on trees in Conservation Areas has to be notified to the council. If the council does not want the work to take place, it makes a Tree Preservation Order to prevent it (see pages 122–4). Demolition of buildings and work on trees without permission or notification in Conservation Areas is a criminal offence so, if you are concerned by buildings being demolished or trees being felled, check with the planning department whether consent has been given. In an emergency, you could try contacting the police to stop unauthorized work being carried out.

The types of development for which planning permission is automatically granted are restricted in Conservation Areas. There are thus limits on 'permitted development' rights for:

- house and roof extensions;
- cladding the outside of houses;
- the size of outbuildings;
- satellite dishes on chimneys, tall buildings or facing roads;
- the size of extensions to industrial buildings; and
- some telecommunications equipment.

Councils can take away other automatic 'permitted development' rights, but only where the particular character of a Conservation Area is threatened by types of development that can go ahead without a planning application (see page 11).

Development proposals in Conservation Areas are looked at very closely by councils to make sure they fit in with the established character. This does not mean development is not allowed, but more emphasis is put on factors such as design, building materials and appearance. District councils can ask for full details of proposals rather than deciding outline planning applications. This applies to sensitive sites where 'reserved matters' – siting, design, layout, access, landscaping – are all important. The careful scrutiny of planning applications can also apply to properties near to Conservation Areas. Proposals outside can still affect the character of the formally designated area. For example, Gloucestershire County Council's proposals for the design and layout of new magistrates courts in the centre of Gloucester were dismissed at appeal, although outline planning permission had already been given. The site was near a Conservation Area and the inspector felt that the design was at odds with the area when looked at as a whole, even though it

FIGURE 7.5 TYPICAL CONSERVATION AREAS

Kempston Conservation Area, Bedford, Bedfordshire

Kempston is in the outskirts of Bedford. The Conservation Area is based on High Street and Water Lane, which retains a village character. Most Listed Buildings at Kempston are in the Conservation Area.

Many buildings are Victorian. Some date from seventeenth century. Pink bricks from local brickworks characterize the area. Water Lane is narrow with buildings of different styles set at varying angles to the road, reflecting its organic development.

High Street has a variety of architecture, including the half-timbered black-and-white King William pub and a group of old stone buildings.

A small copse of mixed deciduous trees at the end of High Street complements the older properties and is a positive feature in the street.

Brunswick Town Conservation Area, Hove, East Sussex

The Conservation Area is based around a number of squares on the seafront. It includes 500 Listed Buildings, more than 100 are Grade I.

Brunswick Square and Brunswick Terrace date from 1820s with designs by Wilde and Busby. The Brunswick Estate was extended in the early Victorian period. Adelaide Crescent, originally designed by Decimus Burton, was completed with the adjoining Palmeira Square 1850–60 by Sir Isaac Lyon Goldsmid.

The Conservation Area exhibits one of the finest examples of Regency and early Victorian architecture and planned estates.

Long Preston Conservation Area, Yorkshire Dales National Park

Long Preston is a village that sits astride the A65 on the edge of the National Park. An important element of the character is the historic network of lanes, which lead to pastures above the village.

The Conservation Area incorporates several outlying groups of buildings that form part of the extended village setting. The area covers twenty-five Listed Buildings, including a fourteenth-century grade I listed church. Also in the area is a scheduled Roman fort and four other sites with known archaeological interest.

was acceptable when looked at in isolation.

When you react to planning applications or appeals for development in Conservation Areas, look up the Local Plan policies. The supporting text often gives a description of the characteristics of the area. Ask at the planning department to see any report or consultation documents drawn up when the Conservation Area was designated. Sometimes the information can be sparse; in other cases, the documents provide a thorough description of the area and identify its important features. Use this to help make your arguments informed, precise and relevant.

Check your Local Plan also to find out whether planning policies give adequate protection to what you believe is important in a Conservation Area. Use the Local Plan process to get additional policies, more specific policies or firmer policies included (see Chapter 5).

LISTED BUILDINGS

Selected buildings and structures are given additional protection beyond normal planning control, because of their special architectural or historic value. Such Listed Buildings are entered on lists kept theoretically by the Secretary of State for National Heritage and Secretaries of State for Scotland, for Wales and for Northern Ireland. More than half a million buildings and structures are listed. They include not only complete buildings but also old-style telephone boxes, medieval walls, train sheds, water troughs, lamp posts and grave stones amongst other structures. Not only is the fabric of the Listed Building covered but also its internal features,

including fixtures and fittings, any other buildings or structures fixed to the building (extensions, coach houses, railings) and anything in the grounds of the building (walls, fences, outbuildings).

Buildings are listed by the relevant Secretary of State after appraisal and investigation by officers of English Heritage, Historic Scotland, the Welsh Historic Monuments Executive Agency (CADW) or Historic Monuments and Buildings Branch of the Northern Ireland DoE Environment Service – the government's advisory bodies on architecture and building conservation. In emergencies, for example where demolition is threatened, buildings can be spot listed. This is a one-off decision rather than listing as part of a wider survey of an area. In similar emergency circumstances, councils can serve a Building Preservation Notice, which provides Listed Building protection for six months. During that time the Secretary of State decides whether to list the building permanently.

Three categories of listing distinguish how important buildings are:

● Grade I, the most exceptional buildings; comprises only 2 per cent of all Listed Buildings;
● Grade II*, particularly important buildings; comprises about 4 per cent of all Listed Buildings; and
● Grade II, buildings of special interest; comprises some 94 per cent of all Listed Buildings.

In Scotland, Listed Buildings are defined as:
● Category A, nationally important; comprises about 7 per cent of all Scottish

Listed Buildings;

● Category B, locally important; comprises about 62 per cent of all Scottish Listed Buildings; and

● Category Cs, good buildings with some element of interest; comprises about 31 per cent of all Scottish Listed Buildings.

There are no separate grades of Listed Buildings in Northern Ireland.

District councils keep a note of Listed Buildings in their area, which you can inspect. The list sets out the address of each building and a short description for identification (see Figure 7.6). The des-

cription might be detailed but does not necessarily define all the important features nor the full extent of what is covered by the listing. This information is not actually given anywhere: planning officers, councillors, planning inspectors and members of the public are left to decide for themselves what special features warrant protection.

Once a building is listed, all work that would affect its special character must have Listed Building consent. Work can be anything from demolition to minor alterations and painting, and it is a criminal offence to carry out unauthorized work.

FIGURE 7.6 TYPICAL LISTED BUILDINGS DESCRIPTIONS IN THE STATUTORY LIST

Country cottage

Late medieval, timber-framed; altered in C17 and more recently. Of two storeys and three bays; formerly having two bay hall to west, but this now floored across. Lower storey of C18 red brick except at west end where original framing survives. Hipped tiled roof; modern casements.

Hotel

Hotel, two builds, north part late C18, south part late C19 and not of special interest. North part painted brick with hipped tile roof. 2 storey, 3 windows, 16 pane sashes in moulded architraves to first floor, 2 tripartite sashes with horns to ground floor. Simple cambered doorcase. Late C18 scrolled wrought iron inn sign fixture. Brick chimney stack to rear. Interior contains heterogeneous collection of architectural salvage.

Town house

House. Early C19, red brick, the south front tile hung on first floor, with tiled roof. 2 storeys, 2 windows. Casement windows with wooden architraves and leaded lights to 1st floor. The ground floor has a right side tripartite casement and left side early C19 bow with 24 panes and reeded surrounds. Off central doorcase having door with cambered head and plank door.

Listed Building applications and consents are like planning applications and planning permission, and proposals that affect the setting of a Listed Building are advertised in local papers and a notice is put up on the site (see Chapter 2). There is also a parallel system of Listed Building enforcement to stop and remedy unauthorized work on Listed Buildings. Applicants can appeal to the Secretary of State.

Both Listed Building applications and planning applications that affect a Listed Building or its setting are subject to particularly close scrutiny. Extra weight is put on preserving the building, its setting and its features. Demolition is not allowed unless every effort has been made to find a suitable use and, usually, the building should have been put up for sale first.

All Listed Building proposals are assessed bearing in mind:

● the importance of the building, its rarity, and the contribution it makes to the area;
● historical interest;
● how well it illustrates past construction techniques;
● the state of repair;
● maintenance costs; and
● whether alternative uses would bring new life to or secure the future of the building.

Decisions on development proposals on or near Listed Buildings turn largely on architectural merits. You can make your own judgments about questions of design, but architecture might be an area in which you need help. Aside from getting professional advice (see Appendix I),

contact local architectural associations or groups involved in preserving and restoring old buildings. They might support your objections. Some district councils have officers who deal specifically with architectural matters and are often called conservation officers. Others use architectural advisers from the county council. Find out who advises the planning officers and contact him to discuss a proposal.

A proposal for eighteen apartment units at the Abbey House Hotel, a Grade II* Listed Building at Barrow-in-Furness, Cumbria was turned down because the layout of historic parkland would have been compromised and urban characteristics introduced into the rural setting of the Listed Building. Similarly, a shop in Henley, Oxfordshire was prevented from putting up canopy blinds on the Grade II Listed Building: the blinds covered up important architectural details and spoiled the simple street elevation of the building.

If you feel an unlisted building or structure, possibly under threat from a planning proposal, is worthy of listing you can request this be done through the district council or local historical or architectural society if it is prepared to take it up for you. Otherwise, you can make the request yourself. Addresses to write to are on pages 145–6.

Westminster City Council planned to demolish the Millicent Fawcett Hall, associated with the suffragette movement, for redevelopment. Campaigners tried unsuccessfully three times to get it listed, but they succeeded eventually. The building was spot listed and was saved from demolition.

ARCHAEOLOGY

Of the 600,000 recorded archaeological sites in the United Kingdom, some 13,000 have, over the last 100 years, been designated Scheduled Ancient Monuments, which gives them special protection beyond the normal planning controls. The term 'Monuments' here covers buildings and structures above or below ground as well as sites with traces of previous existence, remains of vehicles and vessels.

Scheduled Ancient Monuments rank alongside Grade I and Grade II* Listed Buildings in importance and their scheduling is very similar to the listing of a Listed Building (see pages 134–6). The Secretary of State for National Heritage and the Secretaries of State for Scotland, for Wales and Northern Ireland maintain a schedule of ancient monuments that are nationally important. Full details of all known archaeological sites, including Scheduled Ancient Monuments, are recorded by county councils, who have officers dealing with archaeology and advising district councils. Such a Sites and Monuments Record for London is kept by English Heritage and in metropolitan areas it is maintained by the metropolitan boroughs. In Scotland the regional councils look after the Sites and Monuments Record. In Northern Ireland contact Historic Monuments and Buildings Branch of the Environment Service at the DoE.

Once scheduled, Scheduled Ancient Monument consent must be granted for any work involving demolition, damage, removal, alteration, repair or covering up the monument. Some kinds of work, however, are allowed automatically, rather like 'permitted development' (see page 11). Applications for Scheduled Ancient Monument consent are made direct to the Secretary of State. Applicants can ask for a hearing and the Secretary of State can decide to hold a public inquiry but most applications are for minor works and so no hearing or inquiry is usually held. There is no formal public consultation procedure. If a development proposal involves a Scheduled Ancient Monument application and a planning application, any public inquiries will normally take place together.

If planning applications are made in areas where there might be archaeological interest, look up the Sites and Monuments Record map at the county council offices or their equivalents. The fact that a recorded site is affected is not necessarily a reason for opposing development. Discuss the proposal with the county archaeology officer and frame your arguments in the light of this discussion. Consider getting specialist advice if archaeology is going to be the main issue (see Appendix I). It is a criminal offence to carry out unauthorized work on a Scheduled Monument. Despite warnings from the police who were alerted by neighbours, a businessman knocked the top off a brick-and-flint wall in the grounds of a scheduled thirteenth-century castle at Bungay, Suffolk. For this he was fined £3,000.

Areas in which important remains are likely to be found are designated Areas of Archaeological Importance (AAIs). The historic town centres of Canterbury, Chester, Exeter, Hereford and York have so far been designated. Within such Areas, six weeks notice has to be given to the district council of any proposals to disturb the

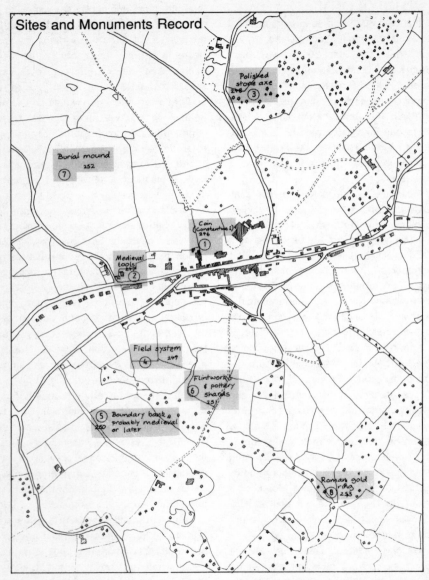

Sites and Monuments Record

Polished stone axe 248 ③

Burial mound 252 ⑦

Coin (Constantine I) 246 ①

Medieval tool(s) ②

Field system 249 ④

Flintwork & pottery shards 251 ⑥

Boundary bank probably medieval or later 250 ⑤

Roman gold ring 253 ⑧

A Sites and Monuments Record comprises a description and assessment of known ancient monuments, a map showing the location of monuments and an archival record of the site – photographs, surveys and excavation reports.

ground, tip on it or flood it. The site can be investigated and the proposed development held up, if necessary, where excavation is needed.

Where development proposals affect sites that might have important archaeological remains, district councils can ask applicants to carry out field evaluations. This is not a full excavation but an initial appraisal by a qualified archaeologist. If development affects archaeological remains, a balance needs to be struck between the merits of the development and the importance and nature of the remains. Applicants and district councils can agree for sites to be excavated before the development is carried out and district councils can include conditions that sites are excavated.

'ARTICLE 4' DIRECTIONS

'Article 4' directions limit the types of building work and changes of use that are generally allowed under the 'permitted development' rules, which provide for a wide range of minor development to go ahead without a planning permission (see page 11). Where such minor development could be damaging, a district council can make an 'article 4' direction, which compels the owner to apply for planning permission. Most 'article 4' directions concern development in Conservation Areas and in attractive areas of countryside (see Figure 7.7). For example, a direction taking away temporary use rights was made at Gartocharn in the Loch Lomond National Scenic Area to stop a 'rave' party taking place. A district council has to pay compensation to an applicant

refused planning permission in these circumstances because he or she has been denied rights given by government automatically to everyone else.

Changes that have already taken place as well as 'permitted development' rights relating to mining, maintenance work by statutory undertakers and emergency works cannot be included in an 'article 4' direction. Each 'article 4' direction specifies the type of 'permitted development' that is being restricted on a particular site, defined area or whole district. All 'article 4' directions must have the Secretary of State's prior approval before coming into effect except for those relating to Listed Buildings and domestic development, fencing, painting, accesses, changes of use and temporary uses, which come into effect as soon as they are made. These then last for only six months – unless the Secretary of State confirms or rejects them in the meantime.

If development concerns you, you can find out if a site or area is covered by an 'article 4' direction by looking at the district council's Ordnance Survey maps at the planning department. The receptionist should be able to show you a copy of the direction documents and the accompanying plan and statement describing the area and the reasons why the 'article 4' direction was needed. If necessary ask a planning officer to explain the effect of the direction and draw his or her attention to the development that concerns you. The Local Plan might have some information on 'article 4' directions in the area.

If you see development taking place, at one particular site or in a sensitive area of town or countryside, that is visually

FIGURE 7.7 TYPICAL USES OF 'ARTICLE 4' DIRECTIONS

Location	'Permitted development' rights restricted
Conservation Area	domestic works – extensions, porches, outbuildings, satellite dishes minor works – fences, walls, gates, accesses painting outside of buildings where appearance would be affected telecommunication equipment *Note* some rights are automatically restricted in all Conservation Areas
Countryside	agricultural development – buildings, alterations, excavations domestic works – extensions, porches, outbuildings, satellite dishes temporary uses of land for 14 or 28 days a year caravans exempt from other licensing camping by recreational organizations *Note* some rights are automatically restricted in National Parks and Areas of Outstanding Natural Beauty
Agricultural land	minor works – fences, walls, gates, accesses agricultural development – buildings, alterations, excavations *Note* used to stop land being sub-divided and in especially attractive areas
Houses	domestic works – extensions, porches, outbuildings, satellite dishes *Note* where house or area is particularly high quality
Nature conservation	temporary uses of land for 14 or 28 days a year *Note* some temporary use rights are restricted automatically in Sites of Special Scientific Interest

damaging or affecting character yet not covered by an 'article 4' direction, speak to a planning officer. An 'article 4' direction is one possible option available to the council to stop it or limit harm, by bringing the development under full planning control.

GETTING PROFESSIONAL HELP

There is a great deal you can do by your own efforts to influence planning decisions. If you follow the steps set out in this book, your contribution could be effective because you will be putting relevant points to the people who matter, at the right time, and in the best way. What you can usefully achieve yourself depends on the time you are able to devote, on the scale and complexity of the planning case and on what forces are ranged against you.

Major decisions that affect your life are taken through the planning system, which is constantly evolving. The professionals deal with these changes every day. Paying for knowledge and experience can represent a valuable investment. In this Appendix we look at when and what help to get and where to find it.

WHEN TO GET HELP

In theory, the planning system is open and accessible to members of the public, yet the reality can be quite different. To many people Local Plans, public inquiries and compulsory purchase orders appear as a mass of jargon, form filling and red tape. You might find help from someone who knows the ropes can save you a lot of headache, especially if the proposed development is large or complex. At no stage in the planning process, however, are you obliged to be professionally represented, but, if there is a great deal at stake, you might want to be sure everything possible is being done to protect your interests.

This could be where:

● your home or business is threatened by a road or compulsory purchase order;
● the value and enjoyment of your property is seriously affected by nearby development;
● your health and safety are put at risk through increased traffic or pollution;
● the future of your community is jeopardized by largescale housing development; and
● your livelihood is threatened.

Specialist knowledge might prove invaluable when, for example, planning proposals concern a Site of Special Scientific Interest (see Chapter 7). Road layouts, traffic models, distribution and movements can be impenetrable to all but experienced highway engineers.

Planning arguments can hinge on very fine points of legal interpretation, involving acts of Parliament, schedules, rules, orders, regulations, directions and policy. Reams of conflicting statistics can be brought to bear by those supporting and objecting to a planning proposal, so use a professional to help with these complex and difficult areas.

If you are busy and do not have a great deal of time to spare, maybe having someone to do part or all of the work is the answer. Investigation, research, surveys and drawing up statements absorb considerable time to do properly and public inquiries can go on for days, weeks or months. Obviously, getting professional help costs money: fees range from about

£40 an hour for self employed planning consultants to some £175 an hour for a large London firm of planning consultants. Professional help could cost anything from £100 for an objection to a planning application to tens of thousands of pounds for a full case to be presented at a public inquiry by a team of professionals. Campaigners against limestone quarrying in Dyfed anticipated spending £30,000 on full professional representation at the public inquiry.

Always ensure you have a written estimated cost for the advice before agreeing to go ahead. Speak to a few firms. Find out what experience they have and contact someone else they have acted for. Ask what they suggest should be done and how much they will charge, and get this confirmed in writing. Fees could possibly be shared if you involve other people in your campaign.

WHAT HELP TO SEEK

You can hand over to a consultant entirely or use him or her for a specific task such as supplying initial advice on a planning application. This might involve just one meeting or even a telephone call to talk about your concerns and get you started in the right direction. The consultant can supply ideas on how to deal with particular issues, go through your letter of objection or statement, suggest a course of action and say what your chances of success are. He can also draw up a letter or statement, the length, detail and, therefore, cost depending on the nature of the proposal and how much you can afford to pay. Such a professional letter does not stop you lobbying councillors, turning up

and speaking at an inquiry or even writing separately yourself.

It might also be worthwhile commissioning a report on the development proposal. The consultant can look into the case – speak to a planning officer, study the Local Plan, research planning history – and report on what chance the proposal stands, the issues involved and appropriate arguments to use.

Where specialist knowledge on, for example, architecture, highways, ecology or archaeology is important to a decision, choose an appropriately qualified consultant. If the prospect of public speaking at a formal inquiry and being cross-examined fills you with horror, you could appoint an advocate – planning consultant, solicitor or barrister – to deal with procedure and cross-examine witnesses, but still speak yourself. Alternatively, use a planning consultant to act as an advocate and give evidence. For major cases, where you have the necessary funds, employ a barrister and witnesses.

If you pass the whole case over to a planning consultant make sure you know at the outset what he is going to do. Ask to see drafts of statements to check before they are submitted and let him know how closely you want to stay in touch with the case.

WHERE TO FIND HELP

When selecting a consultant check that the person you contact is familiar with the complexities involved in your particular planning development. Figure 8.1 features some types of consultant who might be able to help you. In most cases the best person to seek assistance from is

FIGURE 8.1 TYPES OF PLANNING CONSULTANT

Consultant	Areas of expertise
Planning consultant (RICS or RTPI)	general planning advice, planning law and rules, applications, appeals, enforcement, Local Plans, public inquiries; can recommend barristers and other specialists
Highway engineer	new roads, road orders, road inquiries, traffic, highway safety, access
Landscape architect	visual assessment, National Parks, Areas of Outstanding Natural Beauty, countryside, landscape schemes
Solicitor	public inquiries, challenging decisions in courts, complex legal points
Barrister	public inquiries, court cases, complex legal points
Building surveyor	building design, condition, repair, conversion and structure, Listed Buildings, Conservation Areas
Architect	Listed Buildings, Conservation Areas, building design
Environmental consultant	environmental assessment, pollution, nature conservation, visual assessment
Ecologist	wildlife, endangered species, pollution, nature conservation, planting and management schemes
Archaeologist	archaeological remains, Scheduled Ancient Monuments, Areas of Archaeological Importance, historic towns
Surveyor/estate agent	supply and demand for accommodation and land, market trends, occupation of property

a planning consultant who is a chartered surveyor or town planner.

Chartered surveyors are members of the Royal Institution of Chartered Surveyors (RICS) within which there is a specialist planning and development division. Some firms of surveyors have planning departments, others work exclusively in planning consultancy. Chartered surveyors have a wide understanding of all aspects of property and development, beyond the planning system itself.

They tend to have backgrounds in private practice consultancy and adopt a practical approach to property matters.

Town planners are members of the Royal Town Planning Institute (RTPI). Most are trained in and work for local authorities, but some do leave to act as private consultants.

People affected by planning development often turn to their local solicitor. Solicitors' training and abilities, however, are in the law and advocacy – not in assessing the planning merits of development proposals. A survey of planning appeal statements found that those prepared by solicitors were among the least effective. Planning solicitors can play a valuable role, particularly in enforcement cases and at inquiries, and can advise on a suitable barrister for the case and prepare the necessary brief. Some architects also offer planning services. Architects' skills lie primarily in the design of buildings rather than in planning consultancy. There are occasions where architecture is the main issue. In such cases an architect could provide specialist advice.

As with other services, it is often best to find a planning consultant through personal recommendation. Ask your solicitor, surveyor, local estate agent or other professional advisor. Your friends and colleagues may also know of a planning consultant, but be slightly wary of their recommendations because planning is not a widely understood subject. Someone who, for example, designs house extensions might be well known locally but is not the best person to oppose, say, a commercial development proposal in the Green Belt.

Contact local amenity groups to find out if they have used a consultant or, at a local library, look through professional directories or in Yellow Pages under 'Town Planning'. The headquarters of the professional bodies (see pages 147–8) will usually supply a list of suitable practices. If you are looking for consultants in a very specialist field, the professional bodies, or possibly the district council, are likely to be the most informative.

USEFUL NAMES AND ADDRESSES

COMPLAINTS

COUNCILS – COUNTY/ REGION AND DISTRICT

Local government ombudsman

Commission for Local Administration in England, 21 Queen Anne's Gate, London SW1H 9BU

Commission for Local Administration in Scotland, 5 Shandwick Place, Edinburgh EH2 4RG

Commission for Local Administration in Wales, Derwen House, Court Road, Bridgend, Mid Glamorgan CF31 1BN

Office of Northern Ireland Commissioner for Complaints, 33 Wellington Place, Belfast BT1 6HN

GOVERNMENT DEPARTMENTS

Parliamentary ombudsman

Office of the Northern Ireland Parliamentary Commissioner, 33 Wellington Place, Belfast BT1 6HN

Office of the Parliamentary Commissioner for Administration, Church House, Great Smith Street, London SW1P 3BW

INQUIRY PROCEDURE

Council on Tribunals, 22 Kingsway, London WC2B 6LE Tel. 071 936 7045

INSPECTORS/REPORTERS/ COMMISSIONERS

Chief Planning Inspector, The Planning Inspectorate, Tollgate House, Houlton Street, Bristol BS2 9DJ

Principal Clerk, Scottish Office Inquiry Reporters Unit, 2 Greenside Lane, Edinburgh EH1 3AG

Chief Commissioner, Planning Appeals Commission, Park House, 8791 Great Victoria Street, Belfast BT2 7AG

GOVERNMENT ADVISORY BODIES

ARCHITECTURE/ ARCHAEOLOGY

CADW: Welsh Historic Monuments Executive Agency, Brunel House, 2 Fitzalan Road, Cardiff CF2 1UY Tel. 0222 465511

Council for British Archaeology, 112 Kennington Road, London SE11 6RE Tel. 071 582 0494

English Heritage (The Historic Buildings and Monuments Commission for England), Fortress House, 23 Saville Row, London W1X 1AB Tel. 071 973 3000

Historic Scotland, 20 Brandon Street, Edinburgh EH3 5RA Tel. 031 244 3144

Northern Ireland DoE Environment Service, 5 – 33 Hill Street, Belfast BT1 2LA Tel. 0232 235000

Royal Commission on the
Historical Monuments of
England,
Fortress House,
23 Saville Row,
London
W1X 1AB
Tel. 071 973 3500

Royal Commission on Ancient
& Historical Monuments of
Scotland,
John Sinclair House,
16 Bernard Terrace,
Edinburgh
EH8 9NX
Tel. 031 662 1456

Royal Commission on Ancient
and Historical Monuments in
Wales,
Crown Building,
Plas Crug,
Aberystwyth
SY23 2HP
Tel. 0970 624381

Royal Fine Arts Commission,
7 St James's Square,
London
SW1Y 4JU
Tel. 071 839 6537

COUNTRYSIDE/NATURE

Countryside Commission,
John Dower House,
Crescent Place,
Cheltenham,
Gloucester
GL50 3RA
Tel. 0242 521381

Countryside Council for Wales,
Plas Penrhos,
Ffordd Penrhos,
Bangor,
Gwynedd
LL57 2LQ
Tel. 0248 372333

English Nature,
Northminster House,
Northminster,
Peterborough,
Cambridgeshire
PE1 1UA
Tel. 0733 340345

Northern Ireland DoE
Environment Service,
Calvert House,
23 Castle Place,
Belfast
BT1 1FY
Tel. 0232 230560

Scottish Natural Heritage,
12 Hope Terrace,
Edinburgh
EH9 2AS
Tel. 031 447 4784

REQUESTS TO LIST BUILDINGS

England
Listing Branch, Department
of National Heritage,
2 – 4 Cockspur Street,
London
SW1Y 5DH

Northern Ireland
Northern Ireland DoE
Environment Service,
5 – 33 Hill Street,
Belfast
BT1 2LA

Scotland
Listing Branch, Historic
Scotland,
20 Brandon Street,
Edinburgh
EH3 5RA

Wales
Listing Branch, CADW:
Welsh Historic Monuments
Executive Agency,
Brunel House,
2 Fitzalan Road,
Cardiff
CF2 1UY

GOVERNMENT DEPARTMENTS

PLANNING

Department of the
Environment,
2 Marsham Street,
London
SW1P 3EB
Tel. 071 276 0900

Northern Ireland Department
of Environment, Town &
Country Planning Service,
Commonwealth House,
35 Castle Street,
Belfast
BT1 1GU
Tel. 0232 321212

Planning Appeals
Commission,
Park House,
87 – 91 Great Victoria
Street,
Belfast
BT2 7AG
Tel. 0232 244710

Planning Inspectorate,
Tollgate House,
Houlton Street,
Bristol
BS2 9DJ
Tel. 0272 218811

Scottish Office Environment
Department,
New St Andrew's House,
Edinburgh
EH1 3TG
Tel. 031 556 8400

Scottish Office Inquiry
Reporters Unit,
2 Greenside Lane,
Edinburgh
EH1 3AG
Tel. 031 556 8400

Welsh Office Planning
Department,
Cathays Park,
Cardiff
CF1 3NQ
Tel. 0222 823856

ROADS

Department of Transport,
2 Marsham Street,
London
SW1P 3EB
Tel. 071 276 0800

Northern Ireland DoE Roads
Service,
Commonwealth House,
35 Castle Street,
Belfast
BT1 1GU
Tel. 0232 321212

Scottish Development
Department,
New St Andrew's House,
Edinburgh
EH1 3TG
Tel. 031 556 8400

Welsh Office Transport and
Highways Group,
Government Buildings,
Ty Glas Road,
Llanishen,
Cardiff
CF4 5PL
Tel. 0222 753271

PROFESSIONAL BODIES

Archaeologists

The Institute of Field
Archaeologists,
The Minerals Engineering
Building,
University of Birmingham,
PO Box 363,
Birmingham
B15 2TT
Tel. 021 471 2788

Architects

Royal Institute of British
Architects,
66 Portland Place,
London
W1N 4AD
Tel. 071 580 5533

Barristers

Bar Library, Royal Courts
of Justice,
Chichester Street,
Belfast
BT1 3GN
Tel. 0232 235111

Faculty of Advocates,
Advocates Library,
Parliament House,
Edinburgh
EH1 1RF
Tel. 031 226 5071

Local Government, Planning
& Environment Bar
Association,
The Assistant Secretary,
2 Harcourt Buildings,
Temple,
London
EC4Y 9DB
Tel. 071 353 8415

Building surveyors

Royal Institution of
Chartered Surveyors,
12 Great George Street,
London
SW1P 3AD
Tel. 071 222 7000

Ecologists

Institute of Ecology &
Environmental Management,
36 Kingfisher Court,
Hambridge Road,
Newbury,
Berkshire
RG14 5SJ
Tel. 0635 37715

Environmental consultants

Institute of Environmental
Assessment,
Holbeck Manor,
Horncastle,
Lincolnshire
LN9 6PU
Tel. 0507 533444

Highway engineers

Institution of Civil Engineers,
1 – 7 Great George Street,
London
SW1P 3AA
Tel. 071 222 7722

Institution of Highways &
Transportation,
3 Lygon Place,
Ebury Street,
London
SW1W 0JS
Tel. 071 730 5245

Landscape architects

Landscape Institute,
6 Barnard Mews,
London
SW11 1QU
Tel. 071 738 9166

Planning consultants

Royal Institution of
Chartered Surveyors,
12 Great George Street,
London
SW1P 3AD
Tel. 081 222 7000

Royal Town Planning
Institute,
26 Portland Place,
London
W1N 4BE
Tel. 071 636 9107

Solicitors

Law Society,
113 Chancery Lane,
London
WC2A 1PL
Tel. 071 242 1222

Law Society of Northern
Ireland,
90 Victoria Street,
Belfast
BT1 3JZ
Tel. 0232 231614

Law Society of Scotland,
26 Drumsheugh Gardens,
Edinburgh
EH3 7YR
Tel. 031 226 7411

Surveyors/estate agents

Royal Institution of
Chartered Surveyors,
12 Great George Street,
London
SW1P 3AD
Tel. 071 222 7000

OTHER ORGANIZATIONS

Agricultural

Farmers Union of Wales,
Llys Amaeth,
Queens Square,
Aberystwyth,
Dyfed
SY23 2AE
Tel. 0970 612755

National Farmers Union,
Agriculture House,
Knightsbridge,
London
SW1X 7NJ
Tel. 071 235 5077

National Farmers Union of
Scotland,
17 Grosvenor Crescent,
Edinburgh
EH12 5EN
Tel. 031 337 4333

Ulster Farmers Union,
475 Antrim Road,
Belfast
BT15 3DA
Tel. 0232 370222

Appeal decision service

Compass (computerized
planning appeals service),
Suite 3,
Fullers Court,
38 Lower Quay Street,
Gloucester
GL1 2LW
Tel. 0452 310566

Commercial development

Chamber of Commerce –
see Yellow Pages
Directories

Countryside/nature

Association for the
Protection of Rural
Scotland,
483 Lawnmarket, Edinburgh
EH1 2NT
Tel. 031 225 7013

Council for the Protection of
Rural England,
Warwick House,
25 Buckingham Palace
Road,
London
SW1W 0PP
Tel. 071 976 6433

Council for the Protection of
Rural Wales,
Ty Gwyn,
31 High Street,
Welshpool,
Powys
SY21 7JP
Tel. 0938 552525

National Trust,
36 Queen Anne's Gate,
London
SW1H 9AS
Tel. 071 222 9251

National Trust for Scotland,
6 Charlotte Square,
Edinburgh
EH2 4DU
Tel. 031 226 5922

National Trust (Northern
Ireland),
Rowallane House,
Saint Field,
Ballynahinch,
Co Down
BT2 7SE
Tel. 0238 510721

Royal Forestry Society of England, Wales & Northern Ireland,
102 High Street,
Tring,
Herts
HP23 4AH
Tel. 0442 822028

Royal Society for Nature Conservation,
120 Wilton Road,
London
SW1V 1JZ
Tel. 071 931 0601

Royal Society for the Protection of Birds,
The Lodge,
Sandy,
Bedfordshire
ST19 2DL
Tel. 0767 680551

Ulster Society for the Preservation of the Countryside,
2a Windsor Road,
Belfast
BT9 7FO
Tel. 0232 381304

Wildlife Link,
246 Lavender Hill,
London
SW11 1LJ
Tel. 071 924 2355

Wildlife Trusts - see Yellow Pages Directories

Environment

Friends of the Earth,
26 Underwood Street,
London
N1 7JT
Tel. 071 490 1555

Greenpeace (UK),
Canonbury Villas,
London
N1 2PN
Tel. 071 354 5100

London Ecology Unit,
Bedford House,
125 – 133 Camden High Street,
London
NW1 7JR
Tel. 071 267 7944

Historic buildings, Conservation Areas and archaeology

Ancient Monuments Society,
St Anns Vestry Hall,
Church Entry,
London
EC4V 5EU
Tel. 071 236 3934

Belfast Civic Trust,
28 Bedford Street,
Belfast
BT2 7SE
Tel. 0232 238437

Civic Trust (England & Wales),
17 Carlton House Terrace,
London
SW1Y 5AW
Tel. 071 930 0914

Civic Trust (Scotland),
24 George Square,
Glasgow
G2 1EF
Tel. 041 221 1466

Georgian Group,
37 Spital Square,
London
E1 6DY
Tel. 071 377 1722

National Trust,
36 Queen Anne's Gate,
London
SW1H 9AS
Tel. 071 222 9251

National Trust for Scotland,
6 Charlotte Square,
Edinburgh
EH2 4DU
Tel. 031 226 5922

National Trust (Northern Ireland),
Rowallane House,
Saint Field,
Ballynahinch,
Co Down BT2 7SE
Tel. 0238 510721

Rescue The British Archaeological Trust,
15A Bull Plain,
Hertford,
Herts
SG14 1DX
Tel. 0992 553377

Society for the Protection of Ancient Buildings,
31 Spital Square,
London
E1 6DY
Tel. 071 377 1644

Victorian Society,
1 Priory Gardens,
London
W4 1TT
Tel. 081 994 1019

Open spaces, recreation and common land

Garden History Society,
Eton Hall,
Eton College Road,
London
NW3 2DN
Tel. 071 483 0873

National Playing Fields Association,
25 Ovington Square,
London
SW3 1LJ
Tel. 071 584 6445

Open Spaces and Footpaths
Preservation Society,
25A Bell Street,
Henley-on-Thames,
Oxon
RG9 1BA
Tel. 0491 573535

Rights of way & footpaths

Open Spaces and Footpaths
Preservation Society,
25A Bell Street,
Henley-on-Thames,
Oxon
RG9 1BA
Tel. 0491 573535

Ramblers Association,
1 – 5 Wandsworth Road,
London
SW8 2LJ
Tel. 071 582 6878

Roads

Transport 2000,
Walkden House,
10 Melton Street,
London
NW1 2EB
Tel. 071 388 8386

Waterways

Inland Waterways
Association,
114 Regents Park Road,
London
NW1 8UQ
Tel. 071 586 2556

National Rivers Authority
(England and Wales) – see
telephone directory

Rivers Purification Boards
(Scotland) – see telephone
directory

Water Service,
Northern Ireland DoE – see
telephone directory

BOOKLETS AND LEAFLETS

Free of charge from your
local council offices or from:

Department of the
Environment,
PO Box 135,
Bradford,
West Yorkshire
BD9 4UH

● A householder's guide
for the installation of
satellite television dishes;
● Award of costs following
planning appeals: a guide
for appellants;
● Compulsory purchase
orders: a guide to
procedure;
● Development plans: what
you need to know;
● Enforcement notice
appeals: a guide to
procedure;

● Environmental
assessment;
● Land compensation:
your rights explained
(series of five booklets);
● Lawful development
certificates: a user's
guide;
● Outdoor advertisements
and signs: a guide for
advertisers;
● Planning appeals: a
guide; and
● Planning permission: a
guide for industry.

Scottish Development
Department,
New St Andrew's House,
Edinburgh
EH1 3SZ
National Planning Policy
Guideline: the planning
system

Scottish Office Inquiry
Reporters Unit,
2 Greenside Lane,
Edinburgh
EH1 3AG
Planning Permission
Appeals in Scotland

Town and Country Planning
Service, Northern Ireland
DoE,
Commonwealth House,
35 Castle Street,
Belfast
BT1 1GU
Planning Bulletin
(published annually)

Appendix III
GLOSSARY

Advance Notice of Decision
indication of the result of an appeal inquiry given before the formal decision is issued

adverse objection
objection to a Local Plan made to change it in a way that would be against your interests

agent
any representative who acts for an applicant for planning permission, appellant or Local Plan objector

AONB
see Area of Outstanding Natural Beauty

appeal questionnaire
standard form completed by a district council giving details of an appeal that is sent to the Planning Inspectorate and appellant

appeal statement
written case in support of, or opposing, an appeal that is considered by a planning inspector

appellant
an applicant for planning permission who appeals against the council's decision

appropriate development
limited types of development that are allowed in Green Belts: agriculture, outdoor sports, cemeteries, institutions in extensive grounds

applicant
individual or body that applies for planning permission

Area of Archaeological Importance
historic area designated to protect archaeological remains where proposed ground works must be notified to the council

Area of Outstanding Natural Beauty
defined area of countryside formally designated to protect its scenic value

breach of planning control
development carried out without planning permission or without complying with conditions on a planning permission

Building Preservation Notice
notice served by a council giving emergency protection to a building while the Secretary of State decides whether to list the building

called-in application
planning application where the Secretary of State takes responsibility for making the decision from the council

closing speech
summing up of a case at an inquiry by each party's advocate

commissioner
see Planning Appeals Commission

compulsory purchase order
documents showing the land to be bought by an authority, the purpose for which the land is being bought and who owns each part of the land covered

cross-examine
asking witnesses questions at a public inquiry about their cases

decision letter
letter sent to appellant, council and others by a planning inspector giving the result of an appeal and reasons for the decision

decision notice
document setting out the result of a planning application sent to an applicant by the council

delegated decision
decision of a planning application taken by a planning officer on behalf of the council

deferred decision
decision of a planning committee to put off deciding a planning application pending further information or action

deposit draft Local Plan
formal stage in drawing up a Local Plan when it is published and objections and representations can be made

deposit period
time allowed to make formal objections and representations on a draft Local Plan of at least six weeks

developer
individual or body that carries out development but usually used to describe those who develop for profit rather than for their own use or occupation

development control officer
planning officer dealing with planning applications and appeals as opposed to Local Plans

development plan
formal title for both the Structure and Local Plan

district council
local government responsible for a district within a county dealing with most day to day planning matters including planning applications (used in this book to include city and borough councils)

DTp
abbreviation for Department of Transport, which deals with trunk roads in England and Wales

enforcement
collective term for councils' powers to deal with unauthorized development

enforcement officer
council officer responsible for investigating unauthorized development and complaints about development made by the public

environmental assessment
detailed statement required in a limited number of cases on the effects a proposed development would have on the environment that is assessed by a council or inspector in reaching a decision

evidence
facts and opinion put forward by a witness at an inquiry in support of a case

full planning permission
consent to carry out development that includes all details of buildings, layout, access and alterations

Green Belt
land around certain major towns and cities formally designated to stop urban sprawl and protect countryside

informal hearing
procedure for deciding planning appeals

where an inspector leads a discussion about the main issues between the appellant and council

Inquiry Reporters Unit
body that administers the work of inquiry reporters who decide and report on planning appeals and Local Plans in Scotland

inquiry inspector
see Planning Inspectorate

landscape officer
council officer responsible for trees, tree planting schemes and landscape matters

Lawful Development Certificate (LDC)
document issued by a council stating that planning permission is not needed for the development specified in the application

line order
document approving the route or centre line of a proposed section of trunk road

Listed Buildings
buildings and structures recorded in a statutory list given additional protection because of their special historic or architectural value

Local Plan
document comprising maps and a written statement setting out a council's policies for new development and controlling development in its area

local planning authority
council with responsibility for planning, that is county/regional councils and district councils

major development
types of large-scale development for which planning applications must be advertised in a local newspaper

material considerations
factors which should be taken into account in making planning decisions, such as government advice, special designations and the nature of the site and its surrounding area

Minerals Plan
county/regional council's planning policy document for exploration, extraction and treatment of minerals

minor development
types of small-scale development for which planning applications do not have to be advertised in local newspapers

National Park
specially protected area of attractive countryside, with its own authority dealing with planning, designated to preserve and enhance its natural beauty and to promote its enjoyment by the public

National Planning Guidelines (NPGs)
statements of government planning policy for Scotland each covering a particular topic

National Scenic Area
area of attractive countryside in Scotland formally designated to protect its scenic value

neighbour notification
letter sent to people near a site letting them know that a planning application has been made

outline planning permission
consent to carry out development in principle with some or all of the details left to be established later, cannot be given for changes of use, engineering works or mining

parish council
local government body covering a parish within a district, made up of elected councillors who have no legal powers to decide planning applications but often have influence with the district council (used in this book to include town and community councils)

permitted development
types of development given planning permission automatically by a central government order which removes the need to apply for planning permission

Planning Advice Note
statement of government planning policy for Scotland covering a particular topic

planning agreement
see planning obligation

Planning Appeals Commission
body that administers the work of commissioners who decide and report on planning appeals and Local Plans in Northern Ireland

planning application
application made to a council for permission to carry out building work and changes of use of buildings and land; comprises forms, location plan, plans and drawings, certificate of land ownership and council's fee

planning consultant
professional who advises clients on development proposals and planning law, procedure and practice

planning gain
benefit provided for the public by applicant as part of a planning permission, such as road improvements or community buildings

Planning Inspectorate
body that administers the work of planning inspectors who decide and report on planning appeals and Local Plans in England and Wales

planning obligation
legal document signed by a landowner, usually in connection with a planning application, requiring him to carry out or contribute towards the cost of specified work or to limit the use of land and buildings

planning officer
local government employee who carries out the work and implements the policies of the council, gives technical advice to council committees and information to members of the public

Planning Policy Guidance Notes
statements of government planning policy for England and Wales each covering a particular topic

programme officer
person employed by a district council to administer a Local Plan inquiry and liaise between the inspector, planning officers and objectors

proposals map
plan showing the area covered by a Local Plan indicating where various policies apply and identifying sites allocated for development

public inquiry
formal hearing open to the public where cases for and against a development proposal are made and examined by an inspector

re-examine
further questions put by parties' advocates to their own witnesses after cross-examination

Regional Planning Guidance Notes
statements of government planning policy for the regions of England and Wales covering a broad strategy for development

reserved matters application
application made to a council for the approval of details of siting, layout, design, access and landscaping after outline planning permission has been given

road order
see line order and side road order

Scheduled Ancient Monument
archaeological remains or structure included in a statutory schedule, given additional protection because of its national importance

section 106 agreement
see planning obligation

side road order
document approving changes to existing roads and junctions needed as a result of a new section of trunk road

site notice
formal notice put up on a property to publicize a planning application or public inquiry

Site of Special Scientific Interest
area formally designated to protect its particular wildlife or geological features

SSSI
see Site of Special Scientific Interest

statutory plan
Structure or Local Plan that has completed the formal plan-making process and is then given special status in planning decisions

Structure Plan
written document with a key diagram setting out the council's broad development strategy and planning policies for its county/region

TPO
see Tree Preservation Order

Tree Preservation Order (TPO)
document identifying single trees, groups, areas or woodlands that are protected from any work or felling without permission

Unitary Development Plan
planning policy document in Greater London and metropolitan areas fulfilling the functions of a Structure and Local Plan, drawn up by a borough or city council

Urban Development Corporations
bodies set up to help regenerate derelict areas of certain cities, most decide planning applications in their areas

Waste Plan
county/regional council's planning policy document covering land filling, amenity tips, waste transfer and processing waste

Index

Numbers in italics refer to figures.

ROY SPEER AND MICHAEL DADE

Roy Speer and Michael Dade are chartered surveyors specializing in
town and country planning. Both have degrees in Estate Management
and are experienced writers and speakers on planning and property
matters. They run their own practice, where they advise individuals
and groups about development and help people to deal with the
planning system.

Speer Dade Planning Consultants, Premier House, 11 Marlborough Place, Brighton,
East Sussex BN1 1UB Tel: 0273 608311